The New Americans
Recent Immigration and American Society

Edited by
Steven J. Gold and Rubén G. Rumbaut

A Series from LFB Scholarly

The Social Context of Residential Integration
Ethnic Groups in the United States and Canada

Ann H. Kim

LFB Scholarly Publishing LLC
El Paso 2009

Library of Congress Cataloging-in-Publication Data

Kim, Ann H., 1972-
  The social context of residential integration: ethnic groups in the
United States and Canada / Ann H. Kim.
     p. cm. -- (The new Americans: recent immigration and American
society)
  Includes bibliographical references and index.
  ISBN 978-1-59332-347-9 (hbk.: alk. paper)
  1. Minorities--Housing--United States. 2. Minorities--Housing--
Canada. 3. Residential mobility--United States. 4. Residential
mobility--Canada. 5. Ethnic groups--United States. 6. Ethnic groups--
Canada. 7. Multiculturalism--United State. 8. Multiculturalism--
Canada I. Title.
  HD7288.72.U5K55 2009
  305.800973--dc22

                                                           2009035637

ISBN 978-1-59332-347-9

Printed on acid-free 250-year-life paper.

Manufactured in the United States of America.

Contents

Acknowledgements   vii

CHAPTER ONE   1
Introduction

CHAPTER TWO   15
Pathways to spatial incorporation: A comparative framework

CHAPTER THREE   29
A contrast of contexts: The United States and Canada compared

CHAPTER FOUR   47
Metropolitan integration: Data, variables and methods

CHAPTER FIVE   69
Panethnicity and ethnic resources in metropolitan integration

CHAPTER SIX   101
Narrowing the focus: Four ethnic groups

CHAPTER SEVEN   127
Ethnic pathways to neighborhood integration

CHAPTER EIGHT   155
Conclusions: Ethnic integration in comparative perspective

Appendix A: Fourteen ethnic groups in the U.S. and Canada   165
Appendix B: A comparison of census data   185
Appendix C: The question of selection bias   193
References   205
Index   215

Acknowledgements

I have had a longstanding interest in questions about the immigrant and ethnic integration process, and how this is shaped by social, economic and political conditions and institutions in places of origin and destination, social networks and social capital, families, culture, ethnic and racial communities, human capital and motivation, and the context of migration - including immigration policies and international relations. But it is only through this project that I have attempted to do it comprehensively, which has been inspired by observations on the differences between the two countries.

I am grateful for the outstanding support I have had throughout this entire project. Michael J. White, Calvin Goldscheider, and José Itzigsohn were most helpful and insightful throughout the study and on earlier drafts. For moral and emotional support, He Sook Sunwoo, Bong Kyon Kim, Trevor, Jonas and Peter were unwavering.

CHAPTER ONE
Introduction

This study investigates ethnic residential integration in a comparative perspective. In doing so, it aims to address the key question, Are ethnic residential patterns and processes influenced by the national context? It examines whether and how the social and structural context can be important for shaping the spatial configuration of urban areas and identifies several ideological and institutional factors relevant for these patterns in Canada and the United States, two well-known immigrant destinations. By taking residential patterns as one dimension of intergroup relations and social organization, this cross-national analysis of ethnic groups expands our understanding of the contextual nature of ethnic integration patterns and processes more generally.

Finding a place to live is arguably one of the most pressing aspects of settlement for every new arrival. For some, geographic proximity to co-ethnic members may not be a necessary feature of their integration. These newcomers may arrive with pre-existing job offers in particular places, with sufficient knowledge of the official language(s), and they may be on their own, without other family members. For others, geographic proximity to expatriates may be a small comfort in a foreign environment. Family members, friends and new community acquaintances assist with the transition into a local and national community. As a result, these immigrants become identified as members of local ethnic communities soon after their arrival and situate in ethnic neighborhoods, which have endearingly come to be marked by their ethnic theme as "Little Italy," "Chinatown," "Koreatown," or "Greektown." In these residential enclaves, ethnicity is the social glue that binds people spatially.

Yet, residential concentration is not constant across all ethnic groups. Ethnic differences in residential organization are often attributed to group factors. Differences in the demographic and socioeconomic composition of ethnic groups, shaped by successive migration waves, are invoked to account for integration differentials. For example, groups with a large foreign-born contingent might be expected to face constraints in housing choices likely due to limited information and income, which would lead them to ethnic neighborhoods. A cultural perspective may also explain residential propinquity, referring to values regarding homeownership, housing preferences and community solidarity. The distinctiveness of particular groups that have emerged in multiple settings support claims that ethnic residential concentration can be culturally based.

Despite the persistence of ethnic delineations in urban spatial organization and the availability of relatively comparable data, there are very few systematic studies that compare the residential integration patterns and processes of multiple groups in multiple settings. Ethnic outcomes and processes are variable. They are not constant across ethnic groups. Nor should we assume that they are constant for the same ethnic group in different places. In other words, ethnic communities manifest differently in residential terms in different places. A group's experience differs in important ways depending on social ties, reception in local mainstream and co-ethnic communities, and national structures, institutions and organizing principles.

Proximity to the ethnic community may be a strong consideration in residential selection, but the importance of ethnic connectedness for one's social and economic adjustment varies across contexts. Ethnic integration is embedded in larger structural conditions that can shape group relations and the degree of ethnic relevance. The thesis that ethnic outcomes are destination dependent has been gaining theoretical and empirical ground in the sociological literature over the past several decades.

Much of the progress is evident in work on immigrants' economic integration. Work by Jeffrey Reitz and colleagues (Reitz 1998; Reitz, Frick, Calabrese and Wagner 1999) and Suzanne Model and colleagues (Model 1997; Model, Fisher and Silberman 1999; Model and Ladipo 1996) among others (Dinardo and Lemieux 1997; Lewin-Epstein, Semyonov, Kogan and Wanner. 2003; Portes 1995; Tubergen, Flap and Maas 2004; Waldinger 1986; 1989) show that economic outcomes (i.e.

labor force participation, occupation and earnings, self-employment, enclave economies) of immigrant and ethnic groups are related to the opportunity structures and institutional contexts of host societies. Cross-national differences in political and civic participation have also recently caught the attention of comparative scholars, notably Bloemraad (2003; 2006), as have language (Tubergen and Kalmijn 2005) and identity (Foner 1998).

A result of this growing body of literature is the recognition that the sharp dichotomy of culture versus structure in the ethnic integration debate is a problematic construction. Both factors play important roles in the way in which ethnic communities become a part of destination societies. Culture equips ethnic communities with strategies, meanings, values and a repertoire of legitimate actions, which interact with a social structure that either facilitates or inhibits certain behaviors. For this reason, the same ethnic groups cannot be expected to have the identical outcomes in different places nor can different ethnic groups be expected to have the same outcomes in the same place. With respect to residential patterns, one facet of the integration process, the extent to which residential integration is conditioned by the social and institutional structures of destination societies remains open to question.

THE IMPORTANCE OF ETHNIC RESIDENTIAL PATTERNS

Geography operates as a backdrop for social interaction and social and economic outcomes. Cities and neighborhoods undergo succession and change through the behavior of their inhabitants and the decisions of governments and the private sector. All of this points to the dynamic importance of residence and space. In accordance, at least two major motivations appear to influence the study of residential patterns among ethnic groups. The non-random spatial sorting of immigrants into particular sections of the urban landscape gives us insight into society and the place of ethnic groups in relation to one another within it (White and Glick 1999). This is the first motivation. The second is related to the view that place matters and has effects that reach beyond its borders and into other aspects of a resident's existence (Cho, Gimpel and Dyck 2006; Ellen, Mijanovich and Dillman 2001; Ginther, Haveman and Wolfe 2000; Sjoquist 2001; Small 2007).

The persistent separation of ethnic groups over generations has implications for intergroup contact, for immigrant group outcomes and for the cities and countries in which these immigrants reside. The ecological perspective argues that an understanding of the spatial organization of people affects and reflects their social organization. For instance, residential mobility to White neighborhoods is still considered to be an indication of social mobility. But the existence of contemporary middle-class non-White ethnic or racial enclaves suggests that residential concentration can no longer be assumed to reflect status inequality in the same way as income inequality. To be certain, some degree of residential separation comes about through the inequitable allocation of and access to resources. However, a simple picture of socioeconomic inequality across urban space belies the more nuanced process of residential sorting and potential shifts in the meaning of spatial concentration.

The residential patterning of ethnic groups within cities represents their degree of integration or distinctiveness in society. On the one hand, the visibility of ethnic groups within the urban area is suggestive of the salience of ethnic identities and attachments. Having co-ethnic neighbors is one manifestation of a link to the ethnic community – albeit not the only manifestation – and such neighbors offer some protection from the wider community and guide the socialization of immigrants and their children. The common set of understandings, shared language and religion, social networks and the exchange of information are all features that attract co-ethnic neighbors. The values of multiculturalism or cultural pluralism support this kind of residential distinctiveness (Balakrishnan and Hou 1999). In this perspective, the ethnic neighborhood also facilitates the integration and adaptation of newcomers to the new society and acts as a form of adaptation (Lieberson 1963); a way of "fitting" into society.

In addition, residential separation according to ethnic boundaries can also bear upon the formation and intensity of group identities and other ethnic group outcomes. A shared structural position lays the groundwork for the emergence and solidification of group identities and becomes the basis for political claims (Itzigsohn 2004). For instance, those who find themselves in the same neighborhoods because of their shared ethnic origin or what may be perceived as a shared ethnic origin may develop stronger attachments to particular groups or identities. These social identities then, can become the basis for making demands on the state for recognition through political representation and through funding for various programs and services such as community centres, language schools and other ethnic institutions. Residential concentration also provides the setting for the growth of ethnic economies. Most studies of ethnic entrepreneurship show that the growth of ethnic enterprise is linked to residential concentration at the metropolitan level (Light and Bonacich 1988; Portes and Rumbaut 1996; Rekers and van Kempen 2000) and at the level of the neighborhood (Light and Bonacich 1988; Lin 1998; Marger and Hoffman 1992; Portes and Bach 1985; Smith 1995; Waldinger 1994). Opportunities for business enterprise emerge in these ethnic neighborhoods, as immigrants possess specialized needs, tastes and preferences that can best be met by co-ethnics (Waldinger, McEvoy and Aldrich 1990). As a result, ethnic neighborhoods offer an immediate consumer base or a protected "consumer" market for budding ethnic entrepreneurs (Aldrich and Waldinger 1990). Aldrich and Waldinger (1990) point out that residential succession explains this process. As newcomers move into a neighborhood and older residents die or move out, resident businesses will change hands. This opens up an opportunity for new immigrant owners and the ethnic economy burgeons from there (Waldinger, McEvoy and Aldrich 1990). As a consequence, the ethnic neighborhood can create as well as reinforce ethnicity (Yancey, Ericksen and Juliani 1976).

On the other hand, residential patterns also offer a window on interethnic relations and shape social interaction (White and Glick 1999). Stronger attachments to ethnic communities may result in less exposure to others and more limited social interaction and English language acquisition (Min 1990). Therefore, co-ethnic neighbors also indicate with whom one does *not* interact whereas neighbors of a different ethnicity can reflect those you are willing to tolerate or accept. To put it succinctly, the neighborhood can act as a source of "closure" (Kearns and Parkinson 2001). The concept of social distance captures this process and to some extent, drives residential trends.

Whether voluntary or involuntary then, the separation of ethnic groups can lead to restricted social and economic mobility. High levels of segregation for racial minorities were associated with increased concentrations of poverty and disadvantage (Massey and Fischer 2000; Massey and Fong 1990), lower housing values and lower rates of home ownership (Flippen 2001; Harris 1999; Kim 2000; Massey and Fong 1990), higher levels of unemployment and limited access to jobs (Burnley 1999; Darden 1995; Immergluck 1998; Massey and Fong

1990; Stoll and Raphael 2000), and restricted mobility (South and Crowder 1997). In other words, residential segregation is also a form of social exclusion. Residential location has further implications for access to resources and amenities (i.e. schools, parks, shops, jobs, health care, clean air, security) and in consequence, for residents' well-being and quality of life. The growing awareness of the importance of place for social outcomes has lead to increasing attention on neighborhood and regional level variables in multilevel research models and to a more sophisticated understanding of contextual factors affecting social behavior (Ellen, Mijanovich and Dillman 2001; Ginther, Haveman and Wolfe 2000; Overman 2002; Small 2007).

PAST RESEARCH

The study of the geographic concentration of ethnic groups in urban areas has a long history in both Canada and the United States. One of the first thoughts that comes to mind when faced with the question of what makes an ethnic group distinctive in a country of destination is the group's visibility in cities. Although the population size of a group often justifies the level of attention on a group's experiences, geographic dispersion does not draw the same scholarly attention as geographic concentration. Partly due to social networks and the perception of economic opportunities, there has been a general tendency for immigrant groups to settle in "gateway cities" and a considerable tradition of research has been generated on the ethnic groups that emerge in those places; on Cubans in Miami (Portes and Bach 1985), Chinese in New York City (Lin 1998) and Koreans in Los Angeles (Light and Bonacich 1988), to name but a few. The city or metropolitan area is one level at which spatial considerations operate in the study of ethnic integration.

Within urban areas, members of an immigrant community often congregate in particular neighborhoods to be near kith and kin or as a result of inaccessibility to other residential areas. The empirical study of residential patterns within urban areas demonstrates the persistent separation of ethnic and racial groups even over generations in both countries (Alba, Logan and Crowder 1997; Borjas 1999; Guest and Weed 1976; Dawkins 2005; Kalbach 1990; Kantrowitz 1973; Lieberson 1963). Analyses of segregation among a broad range of national origin groups and across panethnic or racial groups reveal moderate to high levels (White, Fong and Cai 2003; White, Kim and Glick 2005; Zhou and Logan 1991). Zhou and Logan (1991) revealed that the Chinese in New York City maintained separation from other Asian groups such as Koreans, Japanese, Filipinos and Asian/East Indians as much as from non-Hispanic whites. White and Glick (1999) also found moderate to high levels of segregation of white ethnic groups such as the Portuguese, Arabs and Ukrainians.

Past studies found segregation patterns could be partly explained by local labor markets, the urban structural context and ethnic group characteristics. In the U.S., population size and composition, the amount of new housing construction and the economic base of metropolitan areas were significant aspects of the urban context for racial segregation (Farley and Frey 1994; Frey and Farley 1996; Iceland and Scopilliti 2008; Massey and Denton 1987; Timberlake and Iceland 2007; White, Fong and Cai 2003; White and Glick 1999).

In Europe, Arbaci (2008) highlighted a number of additional factors at the macro-scale, those related to the welfare system, dual housing systems, host society ideology, and socio-urban policies related to gentrification and renewal, while others pointed to the impact of immigration flows (Musterd and De Vos 2007; Simpson 2007) as well as micro-level factors (Bouma-Doff 2007).

Finally, the level of acculturation, socio-economic status and vintage were ethnic group characteristics that were also relevant (Frey and Farley 1996; Massey and Denton 1987; White and Glick 1999). The results of most of these studies however, are limited to the United States and Europe.

In Canada, particular group characteristics such as social class, education and immigrant composition were generally found to be associated with residential outcomes (Balakrishnan 2001; Fong 1996; Hou 2006; Myles and Hou 2004). However, the degree to which these factors were important varied according to the racial or ethnic group. Finally, the Canadian literature on residential segregation demonstrates that urban context has less of an influence on segregation patterns.

Studies that compared segregation patterns across the two countries have revealed some interesting contrasts. Fong (1994; 1996) showed that Blacks in the U.S. tended to be more segregated than Asians while in Canada, Blacks and Asians were similarly positioned on segregation measures. In more recent analyses, higher levels of segregation among minority groups were also found in the U.S. (Johnston, Poulsen and

Forrest 2007b; Peach 2005; White, Fong and Cai 2003). The processes underlying segregation patterns also differed between the two countries. Although the urban context was important for both places, the effects differed in degree and varied by group. For instance, the foreign-born population had a stronger negative effect on Canada's Asian groups than on those in the U.S. (White, Fong and Cai 2003). In addition, the urban context was more relevant in explaining segregation for Black Americans than for Black Canadians (Fong 1996). There were also differences in the direction of effects for other variables. Median household income of the metropolitan area was not as important for explaining the segregation of Asian groups in Canada but had a negative effect on U.S. groups.

While all of these studies suggest that current ethnic residential patterns not only differ across groups but across contexts, they are limited in at least one of four respects: in the range of ethnic or racial groups; in the number of metropolitan areas; in making claims about the national context; or, in identifying the differential processes of integration. Reception in the host society and the diversity in group characteristics and in the history of urban settlement engender alternate trajectories for immigrant groups. These factors underscore the need for more in-depth comparative work. This study begins to fill this gap by including a large number of ethnic groups and urban areas as well as providing a more focused analysis on particular groups in particular cities.

PURPOSE OF THE STUDY

This work is situated in the literature on ethnic integration that demonstrates how ethnic outcomes are context-based or destination dependent. Our understanding of residential patterns across countries, while expanding, remains limited and this study aims to address the gap by investigating ethnic residential integration in a comparative perspective. It further adds to this literature by comparing residential *processes* across contexts. That is, it seeks to understand how various factors contribute to the sorting of ethnic groups in urban neighborhoods in two different national contexts and to elucidate these processes using selected groups. Moreover, it asks to what extent are patterns the result of ethnic factors (i.e. human capital, social networks, culture) and contextual (i.e. urban structure, institutional context).

The three paths of residential integration that can be identified point to the relevance of ethnic group resources such as size, socioeconomic traits, nativity and length of exposure and cultural norms and values in the kind of integration strategies used by group members. The spatial assimilation perspective posits that residential segregation exists because of disparities in socioeconomic resources and cultural differences between social groups. Immigrants are expected to begin immigrant life in ethnic neighborhoods and as they acculturate and improve their social and economic standing over time, residential dispersion is the predicted consequence. The second pathway, identified as place stratification theory, purports that the dual housing market restricts the residential choices of certain segments of society. Ethnic integration does not take place in a vacuum but, in the context of the United States, in a racially stratified social structure. This accounts for continued residential concentration in spite of socioeconomic and acculturation gains. The ethnic retention approach – the third pathway of integration – recognizes that through deliberate action, group members may actually want to live in ethnic neighborhoods. Ethnic preferences and cultural forces can operate to draw co-ethnic group members together and with increasing resources may actually enhance ethnic group separation. The degree to which ethnic groups follow any of the paths of assimilation, stratification or retention in their adjustment to destination societies may be explained by the setting in which settlement takes place, in addition to cultural inclinations.

In order to address questions regarding contextual influences on the incorporation process, the analysis is divided into two parts. The first part, in Chapters Four and Five, takes one aspect of host societies into consideration, the panethnic and racial structure, and evaluates whether there are cross-national differences in the levels and processes of ethnic residential integration, focusing, in particular, on the effect of panethnicity or race. Fourteen ethnic groups in all of the metropolitan areas of both countries are included in the sample to explore broader associations at the metropolitan level and to compare these associations across countries. This type of analysis is intended to offer a general picture of the effect of ethnic resources on metropolitan residential concentration. The advantage of this approach is that the differences in patterns we observe across the two countries will highlight the structural nature of intergroup relations at this level, giving us a sense of how changes in ethnic resources may contribute to the redistribution of ethnic groups across metropolitan neighborhoods. The disadvantages are that the experience of a given group is concealed within this larger pool of groups and metropolitan areas, and that important and systematic cross-national differences by ethnic group may be obscured. To the extent that ethnic residential integration is a group experience and related to the unique circumstances surrounding its settlement, a more focused study on individual ethnic groups is warranted.

The second part of the analysis, described and discussed in Chapters Six and Seven, complements the first by attempting to resolve some of the issues linked to the pooled analysis. This is done by directing attention to a finer level of ethnic and geographic detail. Here, I focus on the residential integration patterns of specific groups in particular metropolitan areas to examine whether pathways to integration are specific to ethnic groups and urban settings. I examine whether there are systematic differences in the factors that lead to residential distinctiveness for four ethnic groups, Chinese, Jamaican, Iranian and Vietnamese, selected for their contrasting experiences of migration and reception in the destination society, bilateral relations with the respective host society, panethnic or racial grouping and cultural or religious orientation. The metropolitan areas include Los Angeles, New York, San Francisco, Miami, Toronto, Montréal and Vancouver. The disadvantage to this approach is that we do not know whether patterns are particular to these urban cases or indicative of broader, systematic processes.

The main advantage of this bi-level analysis is that we can identify broader patterns and develop an intricate understanding of ethnic integration. Diversity in immigrant characteristics and the context of reception and emigration engender alternate trajectories across national borders. Changes over time in the patterns of immigrant settlement underscore the need for more comparative work at various levels of analysis for understanding the impact of national policies, group migration history and the context of accommodation. The U.S. and Canada share some of the same challenges to attaining social cohesion even though they have undergone distinct journeys. For many developed countries, economic and humanitarian goals of the state have resulted in the continuous movement of people into their respective national borders. With no foreseeable suspension of these flows, the settlement of international migrants and the consequent social and economic interactions that are shaped by this spatial distribution will continue to be of considerable importance to these societies.

LIMITATIONS

There are several limitations to the study but are outweighed by the contributions to be made. The results are not generalizable to all ethnic groups in either country nor to other countries. The processes of residential distinctiveness is also not representative of excluded groups. For the U.S., 29 per cent of the metropolitan area population is represented in the 14 ethnic groups and for Canada, 36 per cent are captured. The four case studies in the second part of the analysis have also been chosen for their unique contexts of settlement. While we may not be able to extend the results to all ethnic groups, we have much to learn about particular groups and we can gain some insight into each country by examining the experiences of those selected. Important contributions will be made to improving our understanding of the mechanisms of spatial organization, the processes of spatial concentration and dispersion, and different structural effects in ethnic group relations.

Second, the statistical analyses use cross-sectional data, limiting generalizability to the contemporary time period. We know that ethnic groups and the social context change over time and the conclusions that can be drawn are not indicative of past or future patterns. Moreover, associations using cross-sectional data are considered to be snapshots of processes that occur over time and these associations are often used to infer causal processes to some degree. However, we must be cognizant that the nature of the data limit such causal inferences.

Third, the units of analysis, the ethnic group and the census tract, are aggregates. There is a risk of ecological fallacy in this type of study and caution must be taken in drawing inferences about the individuals of those groups or in those tracts, although it has been demonstrated that ecological analyses are not completely inconsistent with micro-level analyses (Massey and Denton 1985). Still, inferences are restricted to the group level. Also, we are interested in group effects and the tabular data allows us to address ethnic communities as groups, not as individuals.

Fourth, the social context is often never directly operationalized and this affects to what extent we can have confidence in the mechanisms we theorize. Intercountry differences can be attributed to many factors and any differences may also be attributed to causes we have yet to consider. However, the purpose of selecting two countries that are very similar is to be able to highlight key differences, and to observe whether these differences might play some role. Canada and the U.S. are two countries that share many of the same features but also differ in important ways for ethnic integration. In the comparative framework I identify in Chapter Three, five dimensions are explored; immigration policy, institutionalization of settlement programs, structure of inequality, the housing context, and integration policy and ideology.

Finally, comparisons across countries can be problematic due to differences in measurement. While most variables may appear similar across contexts, there are sure to be idiosyncratic differences in census definitions and questions. Fortunately, Canada and the U.S. are likely to be two of the more similar countries in terms of their census data, and the variables used from each can be assumed, for the most part, to tap into similar concepts. This issue is addressed in Appendix B.

Despite the foregoing limitations, the contributions to be made by this investigation are several: we obtain a much better understanding of the national context on the integration process and ethnic relations; we obtain a better understanding of particular ethnic groups and the conditions under which ethnicity may persist in both societies; we can identify the relative importance of group characteristics and the social context in the mechanisms of spatial integration; the study highlights the degree to which residential integration continues to be an important indicator of distinctiveness; and we can enhance our understanding of conditions under which residential concentration and dispersion take place.

In sum, the results of this research are expected to improve our understanding of the processes and outcomes of ethnic residential integration by comparing the experiences of two different nations. I expect to clarify the degree to which residential patterns can provide a meaningful way in which to understand social differentiation and organization in each immigrant-hosting society. In addition, the comparative perspective will shed insight into the integration experience and its link to the structural and institutional features of the nation-state, ethnic resources and the urban context.

ORGANIZATION OF THE BOOK

This book is organized into eight chapters. Chapter Two details the theories, comparative framework and hypotheses, and Chapter Three compares national contexts, particularly the relevant features of each country that may be considered in residential integration. In Chapter Four, the data and methods used in the first empirical analysis are described. This first phase uses 14 ethnic groups in all relevant metropolitan areas of the two countries, a maximum of 275 in the United States and 25 in Canada. Chapter Five discusses these results. Chapter Six outlines the data and methods for the second part of the empirical analysis of 4 groups, Chinese, Jamaican, Iranian and Vietnamese, each in 2 metropolitan areas of each country, and Chapter Seven presents the findings. The final chapter, Chapter Eight, synthesizes the results of both parts of the analysis and presents some further thoughts and conclusions.

CHAPTER TWO
Pathways to spatial incorporation
A comparative framework

This chapter discusses relevant theories to explain ethnic residential integration and identifies three pathways to residential incorporation. The main objective of this chapter is to establish a framework for comparing ethnic residential organization in Canada and the United States that will guide the empirical analysis.

I review three sets of theories at various levels of abstraction that are helpful for understanding ethnic and racial residential incorporation in urban areas. First, individual or group level theories underscore the resources, characteristics and behaviors of individuals and group members to explain residential outcomes. Second, several dimensions of the urban and regional context are raised, and these are emphasized in the ecological perspective. Third, I examine the relevance of the host societies approach, which argues for macro-scale considerations of institutional structures and organizing principles to place integration outcomes within a wider context. I use these macro-level dimensions to provide a contrast of the two societies in Chapter Three.

THEORIES ABOUT GROUPS (AND INDIVIDUALS)

Three competing perspectives have shaped our understanding of ethnic integration in North America. The first approach, spatial assimilation theory, is the most developed in the residential segregation literature and is extensively applied to studies of racial and ethnic residential patterns. The two alternative perspectives, place stratification theory and the ethnic retention approach, were developed to explain findings inconsistent with the assimilation approach, although the latter perspective does not specifically address residential incorporation. The three perspectives have been conceptualized as separate processes related to individual group members but can also be applied to groups.

Theories of spatial assimilation

The theory of spatial assimilation, derived from the work of Robert E. Park and Ernest Burgess of the Chicago School, explains the process of adaptation by newcomers to a host society (Park, Burgess and McKenzie 1925). Under this perspective, it is expected that newcomers initially live and work within their own ethnic communities but over time, as they become accustomed to the culture of the host society and improve their economic standing they reach social parity with the dominant group. In this perspective, the ethnic neighborhood also facilitates the integration and adaptation of newcomers to the new society and acts as a form of adaptation (Lieberson 1963); a way of "fitting" into society. With cultural and structural assimilation, upwardly mobile immigrants are equipped with the ability to leave and they are expected to do so. Explicit in this definition of social parity is spatial propinquity as residential dispersion from ethnic neighborhoods should be concomitant to rising economic resources and exposure to the host society (Massey and Mullan 1984). Differential locational distributions of racial and ethnic groups are then explained by differences in socioeconomic resources and length of residence.

This theory developed in the context of the immigration of White European ethnic groups to the United States and it has had an immense influence on contemporary studies of residential settlement as spatial assimilation is perceived to be a "necessary intermediate step" in the general assimilation process (Massey and Mullan 1984). However, this perspective has been criticized for its assumption of a straight-line path to assimilation, which has not been substantiated (Balakrishnan 2001; Fong and Wilkes 1999; Kalbach 1990; a 2003; White and Sassler 2000). In the United States, spatial assimilation theory has been generally supported by the experience of Whites and of Latinos and Asians to some extent but not of Blacks (Charles 2003). In Canada, both Asians and Blacks do not seem to adhere to this process of residential integration in contrast to European groups (Fong and Wilkes 1999) although a more recent study using micro-data revealed that spatial assimilation was supported among Blacks and South Asians in Toronto but not for the Chinese (Myles and Hou 2004). The selective applicability of this perspective argues for alternate ways of thinking about residential mobility. The spatial assimilation framework highlights the process of immigrant residential integration and according to this theory, the ethno-national group is the more salient boundary, not broad racial or panethnic ones. However, these concepts of race and ethnicity are confounded in the segregation literature and much of the current research applies the assimilation perspective to large racial categories that do not differentiate among immigrant, or national origins, groups. Thus, the link between ethnicity and race is theoretically lacking. To fill this theoretical gap, an extension of spatial assimilation theory, particularly in regards to racialized groups, is a theory of *racialized spatial assimilation*.

A racialized spatial assimilation perspective argues that immigrants undergo processes of ethnicization and racialization simultaneously. Overlapping cultures, a shared structural position, treatment by outsiders and institutional practices all contribute to establishing encompassing panethnic boundaries. A process of racialization describes the attribution of racial meaning to social groups and stems from the inability of outsiders to identify group members and through racial assignment or racial "tags" (Bashi and McDaniel 1997; Cornell and Hartmann 1998; Omi and Winant 1986). Immigrants not only find themselves lumped into racial categories by way of social interaction but they must also identify themselves racially in governmental and other institutional documents and materials.

Moreover, these broader based markers become internalized by group members. Heightened panethnic identity and consciousness can lead to panethnic behavior such as in political activism, friendships and intermarriage, hiring practices, and residential concentration. Increased social interaction and the building of social networks, perceptions of "sameness," and perceptions about which neighborhoods are friendly and accessible all contribute to shared spatial locations. Members find neighbors with whom they feel they can blend in and they find jobs in longer-standing and more established ethnic enclaves. Ethnic businesses and services that cater to more than one ethnic group also promote this racialized assimilation process.

As a result, we are witnessing the spatial conglomeration of ethnic communities within larger racial and panethnic clusters. And the evidence is pointing to these trends; Chinatowns have opened to other immigrants from Asia (Skeldon 1995), multiple Latin American groups are found in mixed Latino neighborhoods (Pessar 1995; Ricourt and Danta 2003) and West Indian enclaves persist within largely black areas (Crowder 1999). It is from these racial or panethnic clusters that immigrants are expected to experience social and spatial mobility.

Yet, the persistent residential separation of some ethnic groups over time and concomitant to increasing socioeconomic resources have lead to two alternative theories to explain integration processes. These are distinguishable by the degree of voluntarism they attribute to individual group members to choose their residential location.

The place stratification perspective

By neglecting the structural factors and conditions that constrain residential options, the spatial assimilation model falls short in accounting for the residential positioning of ethnic and racial minorities, according to the place stratification approach. This theory points out that ethnic integration does not take place in a vacuum but, in the context of the U.S., in a racially stratified social structure (Bashi and McDaniel 1997). In the place stratification model, discrepancies in residential outcomes are engendered by a racial structure in which members of the dominant group maintain social distance through spatial distance in spite of socioeconomic gains on the part of minority group members. An uneven spatial distribution results from discrimination and racial steering by real estate agents, developers and vendors (Galster and Godfrey 2005; Yinger 1995), and from the avoidance behavior of landlords and local residents, who restrict the ability of members of a minority group to convert individual and household achievements into movement out of concentrated neighborhoods. In this case, the neighborhood acts as a source of "closure" (Kearns and Parkinson 2001). The racialized nature of social organization in the U.S. has lead to continued residential segregation and differential spatial outcomes along racial and ethnic lines. The persistent residential concentration of Blacks, despite ample exposure and increasing socioeconomic resources, is taken as evidence supporting the model of a racial hierarchy (Charles 2003; Heisler 1992).

This model shares a fundamental premise with the spatial assimilation perspective. They both assume that the natural course is for group members to use socioeconomic resources as a way out of ethnic neighborhoods, leading to lower segregation levels. The difference lies in the predicted outcome and explanatory mechanisms; spatial assimilation theory argues increased SES will increase integration due to the adoption of host country orientations and behaviors, and place stratification theory asserts that increased SES will not decrease segregation due to systemic discrimination and residentially endogenous preferences by Whites, a process determined by the position of the racial group. In essence, this difference can be attributed to the extent to which they account for the context of racial inequality. By pointing to the racial structure of society, the place stratification approach argues that the residential choices of certain segments of the population are bound by their membership in a racialized minority group.

The contextualization of residential integration in place stratification theory is an improvement over theories that do not consider the implications of structural conditions. However, the theory itself was developed in a context of Black-White racial inequality and residential segregation, and its limitations are reflective of such. Exactly how and where non-Black and non-White groups fit within the bipolar model is unclear. For the most part, all racialized minorities appear to have been subsumed under a non-White status. However, in the contemporary period, this bipolar conceptualization overlooks the racial experiences of non-Black and non-White groups and a more comprehensive formulation of racial stratification is needed (Gold 2004); all the more so since the racial hierarchy has become more complex than a simple top-down structure with Whites on top and Blacks at the bottom (Song 2004).

The ethnic retention approach

The experience of particular groups provides further evidence contrary to both spatial assimilation and place stratification perspectives, as segregation endures despite high levels of socioeconomic attainment and dominant racial group membership (Balakrishnan and Hou 1999; Kalbach 1990; Logan, Alba and Zhang 2002), and through the voluntary separation of minority groups (Lacy 2004). For some groups then, neither of these explanations may be adequate.

The ethnic retention approach, in contrast to the place stratification perspective, argues that group members can take an active role in creating and perpetuating ethnic spaces. Like the place stratification perspective, it attempts to explain why some groups continue to maintain their distinctiveness well past the time of initial settlement. Although this perspective is not explicitly spatial and has been used to explain enduring ethnic social ties and ethnic identities, it can be adapted for understanding processes of residential incorporation.

This third path of residential incorporation focuses on in-group preferences to preserve the ethnic community in urban space (Logan, Alba and Zhang 2002). The rise in exogenous group contact in some spheres, such as the workplace, may contribute to the effect of increasing or enduring group distinctiveness in others, such as in neighborhoods. For example, Balakrishnan and Hou (1999) found that despite increasing occupational integration over time, residential segregation persisted. This is consistent with the ethnic retention perspective, which recognizes that assimilation or incorporation can occur along some dimensions without diminishing the relevance of ethnicity (Breton et al. 1990).

The ethnic retention approach would argue that through deliberate action, group members may prefer to live in ethnic neighborhoods since they can facilitate the reproduction and transmission of ethnic capital (Borjas 1999). Acting as a centripetal force, ethnic neighborhoods offer communities a means for maintaining and reproducing ethnic networks, identities and values. In this way, residential concentration can be viewed as another strategy to keep social, economic and political resources within the ethnic community.

The common set of understandings, shared language and religion, social interaction and the exchange of information are all features that attract co-ethnic neighbors. They are perceived to be a social good that carries group solidarity and identity, and to provide cultural capital to locally situated group members. Ethnicity operates here as an affective tie that draws co-ethnic members into a shared residential location even into second and subsequent generations and having co-ethnic neighbors is one manifestation of a link to the ethnic community. Such neighbors guide the socialization of immigrants and their children and offer some protection from the wider community.

Part of what contributes to ethnic in-group preferences includes a fear of hostility by others who are not of the ethnic group. Against a backdrop of perceived or actual intolerance and misunderstanding, upwardly mobile group members may look to one another for social support and security from feeling alienated, excluded and culturally peculiar since the experience of racial and ethnic discrimination is not class-based. There is then a premium on living in the ethnic neighborhood, and ethnic preferences for retaining groupness and culture – and avoiding conflict – can promote residential distinctiveness and a pluralistic residential pattern. Through ethnic real estate agents and agencies, the screening of potential buyers by vendors, and information sharing within ethnic networks, ethnic communities can create protected real estate markets.

There has been support for each of these perspectives, with variation by ethnic group. Some of these ethnic variations can be attributed to cultural explanations, where religious beliefs and values with respect to housing take precedence for the residential decisions of ethnic group members. Yet, we know there is more to the explanation of ethnic integration than cultural differences, gaps in socioeconomic resources and the racial structure. As we learned from the place stratification approach, the interaction of a social group with its host environment suggests that the same group may adapt differently in another environment. Structural conditions facilitate or hinder residential concentration by circumscribing opportunities for settlement. Urban ecology and distinctive host society contexts also contribute to the residential sorting of ethnic groups.

THE URBAN ECOLOGICAL PERSPECTIVE

There are variations in the local and regional environments that impact on residential options. The urban ecological perspective provides a framework for understanding how urban structure and organization plays a role in creating unique spatial layouts across cities (Farley and Frey 1994; Fong and Wilkes 2003; Massey and Denton 1987; White, Fong and Cai 2003; White and Glick 1999).

Particular metropolitan characteristics such as population size and composition (i.e. proportion foreign-born, Black or visible minority, elderly, poor), urban economy and housing regimes, and physical housing stock have been shown to play some part in residential patterns (Arbaci 2008; Farley and Frey 1994; Fong 1996; Frey and Farley 1996; Massey and Denton 1987; White, Fong and Cai 2003; White and Glick 1999). For example, the economic base of a city in terms of industry and the spatial location of formal and informal economies may be associated with the type of people drawn into its boundaries and the type of housing and layout of neighborhoods. Newer housing developments would be expected to lead to more integration as they would be less likely to possess any particular ethnic or racial association and residential mobility would be occurring in the context of anti-discriminatory housing policies. The size and composition of the urban area are also expected to have an impact on residential patterns. The size of the metropolitan area may be linked to its age and older cities are more likely to be more segregated. As well, urban differentiation may be greater in larger metropolitan areas resulting in a greater reliance on the ethnic community. The history of immigration would also be expected to impact on the sorting process of ethnic groups as it would determine the mix of ethnic communities and their relative standing within the urban area as well as inter-group exposure. Finally, immigrants have been found to have an impact on local government expenditures (Loveless et al. 1996), which suggests that there should be a reciprocal effect, especially since local governments develop interventions to deal with immigrant settlement and integration. The characteristics of local housing markets and systems, i.e. property ownership, tenants rights, social housing, etc., can also affect settlement patterns. This meso-level conceptualization links the urban context directly with ethnic residential integration.

HOST SOCIETY CONTEXT

Two broad aspects of host societies can be identified. The migration context, or the conditions under which immigrants leave and enter a place, and the way in which they are greeted bear upon the integration process. In addition, the institutional context and the values and dimensions along which a society is organized can be expected to shape settlement patterns.

Contexts of migration and reception

The context of migration includes the reasons and conditions under which emigrants leave one place for another and the political, economic and historical relationship between host and sending countries. Specifically, an ethnic group consisting primarily of economic migrants may likely seek cultural and structural assimilation more so than groups whose histories are characterized by streams of refugees or family migrants. This is in part due to differences in motivations and strategies for social mobility. The context of migration is related to the context of reception. As specified in the work of Portes and Rumbaut (2001), it includes governmental intervention, the pre-existing ethnic community and public opinion. How governments and host society publics respond to newcomers is shaped by the group-specific reasons for in-migration. Where economic aspirations characterize an ethnic group, the group is likely offered little assistance by governments other than in the initial settlement stage and may be characterized as hardworking and diligent by the public and accepted as neighbors. On the other hand, they may be feared and vilified for competing for jobs perceived to belong to the dominant group and separation may be maintained. In contrast, refugees are often offered access to state resources and public support will vary depending on perceptions of legitimacy and awareness of the context of migration. A more favorable climate for residential assimilation can be fostered through state-supported financial and social assistance, and acceptance by the public and the media.

This aspect of host societies suggests that integration is influenced by the specific treatment of and responses to particular groups. A more general view of host societies examines the broader institutional and ideological context for integration.

Institutional structures

To explain differences in the processes and outcomes of ethnic residential patterns across countries, we turn to institutional structures (Reitz 1998) and organizing principles of society (Lipset 1990). At the national level, there is an innumerable list of dimensions along which nation-states can be compared and at least five are implicated in ethnic residential integration. As ethnic group outcomes are strongly linked to the incorporation of immigrants, this conceptual formulation draws from the literature on host societies (Reitz 1988; 1998; 2003). For the residential settlement of ethnic groups, I consider five dimensions: immigration policy; settlement programs and social welfare regimes; integration ideology and policy; the structure of inequality; and housing policy and incentives.

Immigration policy regulates and influences the composition of migrant flows. These flows, in turn, determine the growth and characteristics of the ethnic community and its internal dynamic as well as its orientation to the host society. Immigration policies can vary according to their stated goals and purpose, selection criteria and processes, humanitarian objectives, and obligations for sponsors. The degree to which settlement intervention is institutionalized and seen as a responsibility of the welfare state presents a context for comparing the integration outcomes of ethnic communities. States differ in their level of official support for settlement services and in their expectations of civil society.

To the extent that settlement assistance eases the integration process and allows ethnic group members to find jobs, health care and educational opportunities faster, a greater degree of involvement by the host country would be associated with access to information external to the network and a greater ability to locate housing away from the ethnic community. The use of informal networks over more institutionalized settlement services may result in ethnic group members steering co-ethnics toward their respective ethnic neighborhoods and result in higher degrees of residential distinctiveness, which again would be more prominent in new arrivals.

In addition to settlement services and welfare regimes, countries also vary in terms of their integration ideology and policies and expectations related to social cohesion and "successful" immigrants. Citizenship policies, multiculturalism policies, the framing of immigrants as criminals or terrorists, the discourse of belonging and exclusion, and utilitarian expectations of economic achievement all shape immigrant insertion experiences on different sides of geo-political borders.

The structure of inequality also shapes ethnic interaction in both societies. Reitz (2003) argues that racial and ethnic relations in host societies is a key dimension for incorporation as it frames social interaction and affects the orientation of newcomers. The diversity of ethnic and racial groups and their socioeconomic and political location within society provide a setting in which new groups or group members can situate. A greater degree of racial and ethnic inequality in a society is likely to be reflected in its residential patterns. Arguably, other aspects of inequality such as gender and class can also be relevant and give rise to particular opportunities and social structural conditions for residential mobility. The place stratification approach explicitly accounts for this dimension in explaining the residential segregation of racial minorities.

Housing-related issues are a fifth dimension of the national context that provides a backdrop for the residential integration of ethnic groups. The institutional structure of housing policies and the development and promotion of anti-discriminatory legislation may have some impact on the behavior of landlords, vendors and real estate agents. Moreover, the availability of owned versus rental housing, affordable housing, the spatial locations of social housing, and the degree of homeownership and of residential mobility are important as well.

Homeownership and residential mobility have both cultural and economic facets (in as much as housing is a valued commodity) and reflect social mobility and status. In countries where homeownership is highly desirable, a greater degree of ethnic integration may be likely, especially if group members are eager to move out of immigrant neighborhoods that are characterized by a high concentration of rental units. However, this is not likely to occur for all groups given the growth of ethnic neighborhoods out of central areas and in suburbs (Alba, Logan and Crowder 1997; Zhou and Logan 1991).

WHY COMPARE RESIDENTIAL PATTERNS ACROSS COUNTRIES?

"Canadians and Americans will never be alike, but Americans can learn more about Canada, and Canadians can learn more about why Americans are as they are. And by so doing they will come to understand their own countries better" (Lipset 1990: 227).

In his book, *Continental Divide: The Values and Institutions of the United States and Canada*, Seymour Martin Lipset (1990) compares the United States and Canada and exemplifies how we learn about one country by studying and comparing it to another. The geo-political proximity of Canada and the U.S. provides the opportunity for comparative work between the two places (Table 2.1). They are both highly urbanized, predominantly English-speaking countries characterized by a history of European settlement, present-day capitalist market economies, democratic political systems and meritocratic ideals, and marked by religious, cultural, regional, class and ethnic and racial heterogeneity. They also repealed national-origins provisions in their respective immigration policies in the 1960s. Their continued high rates of immigration raise similar issues of social cohesion and economic integration, citizenship, ethnic relations, social mobility and border control. Finally, neither ethnic residential concentration nor dispersion is directly supported through state legislation. However, both are supported indirectly; integration through anti-discriminatory housing policies and residential distinctiveness with family sponsorship provisions in immigration policies.

Table 2.1 A comparison of the United States and Canada

	U.S.	Canada
Similarities		
	Capitalist market economy	
	Democratic political system	
	Meritocracy	
	Highly urbanized	
	Religious, cultural, regional, ethnic/racial, class	
	History of European settlement	
	"Open" immigration in 1960's	
Differences		
Immigration policy		
	Sponsorship	Selective
Integration programs		
	Laissez-faire integration	Settlement industry
Ideology of integration		
	Melting pot	Mosaic
Predominant immigration flows		
	Latin American	Asian
Position in global economy		
	Lead power	Middle power

Despite these commonalities, the U.S. and Canada also differ in significant ways. They have undergone different historical trajectories and occupy different positions in the global political economy leading to nation-specific bilateral relationships and distinct value (political) orientations and institutional systems. In the context of these differences, group relations do not take on the same meaning or pattern within each country. The integration of ethnic groups occurs within a particular institutional and ideological milieu and cross-national comparisons allow us to highlight its relevance. We have moved beyond thinking of the ability of groups and group members as the sole determinant of immigrant and ethnic integration. We can now examine the impact of the cultural and structural organization of host societies.

In addition, ethnically plural cities all over the world now face the issue of ethnic integration within the urban social, economic and political context. There is a pressing need for comparative studies to explore ethnic residential divisions in different cultural contexts (Poulsen, Johnston and Forrest 2002). In an era of the global movement of people, goods and capital, and an increasing number of immigrant hosting societies, comparative studies are becoming not only possible but essential. We have much to learn about ethnic groups, urban diversities and inequalities, and the impact of national approaches to integration.

CHAPTER THREE
A contrast of contexts:
The United States and Canada compared

In light of the theoretical and conceptual discussion in the previous chapter, this chapter offers a contrast of the institutional and ideological contexts of the U.S. and Canada, mostly related to welfare regimes, and focuses on immigration policy, settlement programs, integration ideology, the structure of inequality and housing policies and systems.[1]

Within this comparative framework and the dimensions contrasted, it identifies three possible paths to incorporation for ethnic groups, assimilation, retention and stratification, and proposes some hypotheses to be tested in subsequent chapters.

IMMIGRATION POLICY

Immigration policy is the tool of the state for specifying eligibility not only for the legal entry of those born on the outside, but also for building a pool of future citizens and for defining who is "desirable." Immigration policies in the United States and Canada share some common elements, which should be expected given the social, geographic, economic and political proximity of the two countries and given that immigration policy does not develop in a vacuum but is linked to other social and economic policies (Simmons 1999) and to the immigration policies of other countries, in a sense being "globalized" (Bashi 2004).

In the 1960s, both countries repealed provisions that essentially

---

[1] It should be noted at the outset that while I accentuate the differences between the two countries, they are likely to fall closer to one another than to others if placed along a more complete spectrum.

limited immigration to those from Europe. Since then, they have been experiencing a "new immigration," or increasing immigration from Africa, Asia and Latin America. Both countries also have provisions for the sponsorship of family members, economic class immigrants (including investors), and for the inclusion of asylum-seekers.

Along with these cross-national similarities, differences in immigration policies have also been noted and I highlight 4 key areas: the goal and stated purpose of the immigration policy; the selectivity of the policy; the scale of international migration relative to the total population; and sponsorship provisions and requirements.

U.S. immigration policy has been characterized as playing more of a gatekeeping role (Boyd 1976; Schmidt 2007). This is no more evident than in the fact that, since 2003, government immigration agencies have been located in the *Department for Homeland Security*. Prior to that, responsibilities for enforcing immigration laws and controlling the entry of visitors fell to the *Immigration and Naturalization Service* (Smith 1998). With respect to legislation and to stated goals, the U.S *Immigration and Nationality Act* of 1952 asserts no specific goals or objectives.

In Canada, immigration has primarily been linked to economic development (Boyd 1976) and nation-building (Simmons 1999) and potential migrants are awarded points for their human capital. The relevant statute, the *Immigration and Refugee Protection Act*, which came into effect in June 2002, states eleven objectives related to immigration, and eight additional objectives related to refugees. For immigrants, the first objective - *to permit Canada to pursue the maximum social, cultural and economic benefits of immigration* – along with three others (*to enrich and strengthen the social and cultural fabric of Canadian society while respecting the federal, bilingual and multicultural character of Canada; to support and assist the development of minority official languages communities in Canada; to support the development of a strong and prosperous Canadian economy, in which the benefits of immigration are shared across all regions of Canada*), demonstrate how immigration in Canada is framed according to its potential contributions.

Historically, immigration in Canada fell to the responsibility of the *Department of Manpower and Immigration* and currently falls to *Citizenship and Immigration Canada* (CIC). The differences in the orientation of immigration policies and enforcement are partly the result of the contiguous border between U.S. and Mexico and the proximity of the U.S. to the Caribbean and Latin America. This has the U.S. government contending with undocumented migrants, more so than in Canada.

This would suggest that the more selective and economically oriented Canadian policy over the U.S. policy would result in different groups and group compositions. Some of this difference can be observed in the types of flows, 69 per cent of legal immigrants to the U.S. in 2000 were family migrants as opposed to the 27 per cent of migrants to Canada in 2001. But it does not appear to lead to more highly skilled ethnic communities in Canada compared with the U.S. Specifically, ethnic groups in Canada should possess higher levels of human capital over their American counterparts. Yet, this does not appear to be the case (Reitz 1998). In fact, 13 out of 14 ethnic groups included in this study had higher levels of education in the U.S. compared to their counterparts in Canada (see Appendix A). Rather, what is more striking is the lack of importance of immigration policies for both immigrant composition and incorporation (Reitz 2003), no doubt an unintended consequence of the contradictions in migration control in an era of increasing globalization and transnationalism (Castles 2004).

Another key difference between Canada and the U.S. lies in the flows of immigrants received in each country as a proportion of the total population. Although the U.S. receives the largest numbers in magnitude, immigrants comprise a much higher proportion of the Canadian population than the U.S. Almost 20 per cent of Canadians are foreign-born compared with 11 per cent foreign-born in the U.S. The scale of immigration in Canada relative to the overall population is thus higher and has a greater impact on local areas that attract most of the immigrants.

A second policy-related aspect is the issue of sponsorship. Both Canada and the U.S. have policy provisions for citizens and permanent residents to sponsor eligible family members. These provisions, which change from time to time in the list of eligible relatives, carry particular obligations on the part of sponsors, particularly in terms of financial assistance, and sponsors have a duty to ensure their sponsored family members do not become public charges or rely on governmental assistance.

In the U.S., citizens are currently able to sponsor a wider range of family members than permanent residents, including spouses, unmarried children under 21 years of age, parents, adult unmarried children, married children and siblings in descending order of preference. For U.S. permanent residents, sponsorship is limited to spouses and unmarried children of any age. According to the policy, sponsors are financially responsible until the family member becomes a U.S. citizen or has accrued a certain number of work credits – equivalent to about 10 years.

In Canada, citizens and permanent residents 18 years and older presently have the same rights for sponsoring family members under the family class, and spouses, common-law or conjugal partners and dependent children under the age of 22 years take priority. The list of additional relatives is broader than in the U.S. and includes parents, grandparents, and orphaned siblings, nieces, nephews and grandchildren under age 18 years, among others. The sponsorship period of financial responsibility ranges from 3 to 10 years depending on the family member being sponsored. Canada's program also goes further by allowing private organizations and individuals to sponsor asylum-seekers.

Immigration in Canada then, is viewed in terms of its contributions to Canadian society, has a greater impact on its existing population than in the U.S. due to its relative scale, and has comparatively more liberal sponsorship regulations.

SETTLEMENT PROGRAMS

Reflecting their social welfare values and those regarding state intervention and responsibilities, the two countries have somewhat different approaches to the settlement of immigrants and their degree of intervention in facilitating integration (Bloemraad 2006; Schmidt 2007). Canada's "newcomer settlement industry," symbolically and materially supported by governments at all levels (Bloemraad 2003), means that newcomers can rely on formal institutions to assist with language instruction and cultural orientation, with gaining access to employment, educational and re-training opportunities, housing, health services, and to keep them informed of their rights and duties among additional programs and services. Schmidt (2007) characterizes Canada's approach to settlement as comprehensive in scope and proactive as it encompasses the economic, cultural, social and political dimensions of life in Canada.

In contrast, the U.S. stance toward immigrant integration has generally been characterized as "laissez-faire," as governments are not perceived to have a responsibility for fostering integration and individuals are generally left to market forces (Kurthen 1997; Schmidt 2007; see Harles (2004) for an alternate perspective). There is an expectation by the state that immigrants will adapt on their own, with the help of family and friends, or with the assistance of voluntary agencies. The state's role is not to facilitate settlement but to maintain control and security over the borders, i.e. gatekeeping (Schmidt 2007). These differences in approaches to immigrant settlement leads Schmidt (2007) to describe the immigration climate in the U.S. as "chilly" while in Canada, it is perceived to be "immigrant-friendly" and "warmer."

The greater reliance on informal networks for newcomers to the U.S. suggests that information on housing and neighbourhoods in particular is likely to be limited within the boundaries of the ethnic community resulting in less residential integration.

INTEGRATION POLICY AND IDEOLOGY

Related to policies of immigration and settlement, countries differ according to how they believe individuals and groups should relate to one another and to the state. The ideology and policies of integration for immigrants and non-immigrants provide a set of values and beliefs about intergroup contact and through national symbols, integration policies and programs, and official statements, states promote normative expectations for group relations. Cross-national differences are an outcome of differences in the historical development of countries and are the result of past strategies used to deal with racial and ethnic diversity and immigration.

While Canada and the United States are both characterized by liberal citizenship regimes (they offer citizenship through naturalization (generally after 5 years of permanent residence in the U.S. and 3 years in Canada), the two countries differ in the degree to which immigrants actually take up citizenship as well as in the degree to which official discourse promotes the rights of ethnic groups to maintain a collective identity and institutions, and to which these are backed by the state.

Immigrants in the U.S. are less likely to naturalize than immigrants in Canada despite the greater benefits of citizenship over permanent residency in the U.S. (Bloemraad 2006). And it is precisely those immigrants from non-traditional source countries who naturalize at the highest rates in Canada, but not in the U.S. (Kymlicka 1998). This gap between the countries has been attributed to the differences in governmental intervention in settlement and managing diversity, with the most emphasis and attention falling on Canada's multiculturalism policy (Bloemraad 2006; Kymlicka 1998). The U.S. does not have an official policy of multiculturalism and instead has been characterized as promoting the melting pot ideal of assimilation, fostered by the belief that ethnic distinctions should disappear over time and that newcomers should renounce their old loyalties in order to become "American." This is no clearer than in the U.S. Oath of Citizenship taken by those naturalized. It reads:

"I hereby declare, on oath, that I absolutely and entirely renounce and abjure all allegiance and fidelity to any foreign prince, potentate, state, or sovereignty, of whom or which I have heretofore been a subject or citizen;

that I will support and defend the Constitution and laws of the United States of America against all enemies, foreign and domestic;

that I will bear true faith and allegiance to the same;

that I will bear arms on behalf of the United States when required by the law;

that I will perform noncombatant service in the Armed Forces of the United States when required by the law;

that I will perform work of national importance under civilian direction when required by the law;

and that I take this obligation freely, without any mental reservation or purpose of evasion;

so help me God."

The U.S. coat of arms, also demonstrates this ideal stating in Latin, "From many, one" and popular media portrayals of immigration and immigrants are a contemporary bulwark for this national canon (Chavez 2001).

In contrast, the position on group rights is stronger in Canada with its bi-cultural colonial history and official policy of multiculturalism, which it was the first country to adopt (Kymlicka 1998). The multiculturalism policy formally recognizes the rights of groups and individuals to preserve their ethnic heritage and customs. Commonly referred to as a mosaic, Canadian public institutions promote the idea that ethnic groups can maintain some degree of ethnic distinctiveness and that they can adopt a new national identity without shedding their old one. The Canadian Oath of Citizenship does not require immigrants to relinquish their transnational attachments:

> "I swear (or affirm) that I will be faithful and bear true allegiance to Her Majesty Queen Elizabeth the Second, Queen of Canada, Her Heirs and Successors, and that I will faithfully observe the laws of Canada and fulfil my duties as a Canadian citizen."

Pluralism is also visible in the Canadian coat of arms, in which four countries are represented, England, Scotland, Ireland and France.

Images of the melting pot and mosaic are contested in each country and there is evidence of the Anglo-conformity model in Canada and the pluralism model in the United States. Recent efforts to officially recognize racial diversity in the U.S. is especially noticeable (Kim 2004). Yet, assimilation continues to be the model backed by the U.S. state and multiculturalism by the Canadian state (Peach 2005). Whether and how state symbols and policies have a direct bearing on the behavior of individuals and groups is debatable. The findings presented in this study should provide some insight to this question with respect to residential patterns.

STRUCTURE OF INEQUALITY

A comparison of contexts is incomplete without some consideration of how countries and public opinions treat minority groups including women, indigenous peoples, racial and ethnic minorities, gays and lesbians, those in poverty and those with disabilities. Both countries have had long histories of exclusionary immigration policies aimed at restricting the entry of Blacks and other ethnic and racial minorities and in their immigration policies have used "non-racial language to achieve similarly racialized ends" (Bashi 2004: 585). In Canada, for example, this has included literacy tests (McLean 2004). Yet, the prominent history of Black slavery and of legitimized racial segregation in the U.S. contribute to a society where race is a key stratifying feature of the American landscape, potentially more so than in Canada (although Canada has its own history of racial oppression and slavery, see Winks

(1971)). The stronger presence of Blacks, in demographic terms (12 per cent) in the United States and in its dominant urban centres undoubtedly heightens the awareness of racial polarization. Canada's Blacks have a relatively small presence comprising approximately 2 per cent of the national population compared with an Asian population of 9 per cent. Canada's history of colonialism has also been more associated with Aboriginal Peoples and English/French relations than a history of conflict between Blacks and Whites.

Reitz and Breton (1994) have attempted to show that this contrast is likely to be more of an illusion than based on reality. They argue that in both places, overt racism is uncommon and that social distance between racial minorities and other groups is on the decline. They also show that in both places, public opinion asserts that minorities are responsible for their own inequality. They do, however, concede that social distance has been smaller in Canada than in the U.S.

Adams (2003) has offered a more recent analysis comparing public opinions on the two sides of the border. He argues that rather than becoming more similar, people in Canada and the U.S. are moving in opposite directions. Citing results from three different polls taken in both countries, he shows that a greater proportion of U.S. residents than those in Canada agreed with the statement that "non-whites should not be allowed to immigrate to this country" with the largest gap occurring in the latest wave in the year 2000, with 13 per cent in Canada and 25 per cent in the U.S. He also cited another poll, which was conducted in 2002, that found 43 per cent of respondents in the U.S. indicated that immigrants were "bad" for their country in contrast to the 18 per cent of respondents in Canada.

In yet another poll in 2003, we observe a greater proportion of respondents in Canada compared to respondents in the U.S. in agreement with the idea that immigration to their respective countries should be increased, that immigrants were generally good for the economy, that immigrants did not take jobs away from people born in the country, and that immigrants made the country more open to new ideas and culture (Simon and Sikich 2007). At the same time, a similar proportion of respondents in both countries felt that immigrants did not increase crime. The results of these numerous polls indicate that the U.S. and Canada are converging in some respects, with the U.S. gradually becoming more favorable to immigrants, but there continues to be noticeable gaps.

Class and gender inequality also permeates both countries. While they are capitalist market economies and accept, to some degree, income inequality as a basis for differentiation, the gap in income inequality is more severe in the U.S. than in Canada due to greater redistributive policies in Canada. The Human Poverty and GINI indices from the *United Nations Development Programme (UNDP) Human Development Indices 2008* in Table 3.1 support this characterization.

Gender inequality offers another context for understanding social, economic and political integration of immigrants. The opportunities open to women and to men differ and to the extent that immigration is a gendered process, ethnic group outcomes will also be affected. Also shown in Table 3.1, Canada ranks higher than the U.S. on the two indices of gender equality and empowerment, thus outperforming the U.S. Finally, with respect to gay rights, Canada recognizes same-sex couples and their right to marry across the country. In the U.S., this right varies by state (Andersen and Fetner 2008).

Overall, Canada outperforms the U.S. in terms of the human development measures offered by the UNDP, ranking 3rd compared to 15th for the U.S. out of all of the high human development countries. While caution must be taken in cross-national comparisons using these indices, it does suggest to some degree that people in the U.S. compared to Canada, including immigrants, live in an environment comparatively less conducive to developing to their "fullest potential."

Table 3.1 Comparing inequality in the U.S. and Canada

Indicators	U.S.	Canada
Human Development Index (rank)	15	3
Gender-Related Development Index (rank)	16	4
Gender Empowerment Measure (rank)	15	10
Human Poverty Index (rank)	17	8
Income Inequality (GINI Index)	40.8	32.6

Source: UNDP Human development indices: A statistical update 2008

HOUSING CONTEXT

Both countries have created institutional structures to deal with housing discrimination. In terms of housing policy, the United States has a national housing policy in the Fair Housing Act that prohibits discrimination in the sale, rental or financing of homes. Housing discrimination complaints go directly through this agency. In contrast, there is no national level anti-discriminatory housing policy in Canada. Rather, this is deemed to be covered under the Multiculturalism Act of 1988, which states:

> "The Government of Canada recognizes the diversity of Canadians as regards race, national or ethnic origin, colour and religion as a fundamental characteristic of Canadian society and is committed to a policy of multiculturalism designed to preserve and enhance the multicultural heritage of Canadians while working to achieve the equality of all Canadians in the economic, social, cultural and political life of Canada."

The federal housing body, the Canada Mortgage and Housing Corporation, ensures housing policies are harmonious with this policy (CMHC 1995). More specific anti-discrimination policies and enforcement are decentralized and fall within the jurisdiction of provincial Human Rights Commissions (the Canadian Human Rights Commission deals with discrimination in employment and services within the federal jurisdiction) where complaints of housing discrimination can be made.

As a means to upward mobility, homeownership may encourage integration as members of ethnic groups seek homes for purchase outside the ethnic neighborhood. The vast majority of housing stock in both countries operates through a private market system and homeownership is highly valued. Canada and the United States have similar rates of homeownership, 65.8 per cent in the former and slightly higher in the latter, at 66.2 per cent.

A final aspect of the context of housing is residential mobility and the degree to which there may be differences in opportunities and in the "culture of moving." In places where residents rarely move, thus maintaining existing and established ethnic residential patterns, segregation may be a more likely consequence. The 2001 Canadian census reveals that Canadian residents move less in a 5-year period than their U.S. counterparts (39.8 and 44.3 per cent, respectively).

IMPLICATIONS FOR RESIDENTIAL INTEGRATION

In essence, the 5 dimensions show that given differential national structures and reception of ethnic groups, we should expect to find that the same groups fare differently in different places. A clear direction of residential integration is difficult to predict in the context of these national differences as various dimensions within a structural context could lead to divergent outcomes and processes. However, some propositions can be put forward.

First, the greater proportion of family migrants that immigrate to the U.S. suggests that this would have a concentrating effect on ethnic communities as opposed to the economically oriented Canadian immigration policy.

Second, the more formalized settlement sector in Canada is also likely to lead to residential dispersion although a counterargument would contend that concentration could result to the extent that settlement services direct newcomers to their respective ethnic communities. A direction is clearer in the U.S. case where the more informal nature of settlement is likely to lead to residential concentration as group members rely on social networks to find jobs, homes and information about services.

The third area, the structure of inequality, is likely to lead to concentration in the U.S. in contrast to dispersion in Canada due to the more racially divided nature of U.S. society.

It is unclear in which direction the housing context would affect residential patterns. On the one hand, the centralized system in the U.S. may result in increased concentration due to individuals' reluctance to approach a national organization and the bureaucracy involved in having a complaint investigated. The more decentralized system in Canada may be less of an administrative deterrent for individuals who wish to approach the agency leading to better enforcement and greater integration. On the other hand, the more awareness and institutional resources devoted to promoting anti-discrimination in housing in the U.S. may lead to greater levels of dispersion than in Canada.

Finally, the assimilation paradigm in the U.S. could only be expected to encourage the residential dispersion of ethnic group members. This is in contrast to the pluralism orientation, which gives ethnic groups the political power to maintain localized ethnic spaces. This summary shows that the U.S. national context, in general, is more likely to lead to the concentration of its ethnic groups compared to the Canadian context. It must be remembered that we are comparing patterns across the two societies and patterns of concentration or dispersion in one place is taken in relation to patterns in the other. The next section describes the three pathways for residential incorporation that can occur within any given context and poses some hypotheses to be tested in subsequent chapters.

Figure 3.1 A model of ethnic residential integration

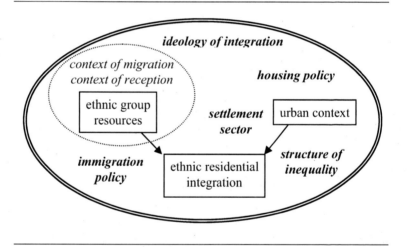

Based on the foregoing theoretical discussion, a visual diagram can be used to illustrate this conceptual framework (Figure 3.1). The model of ethnic residential integration shows that ethnic resources, shaped by the context of migration and reception of a given group, has a direct effect on residential patterns as does the urban context. The five dimensions of the host society are set as a backdrop for the residential processes occurring within its national borders. These five dimensions, in addition to the context of migration and reception, argue for a cross-national perspective in the study of ethnic integration.

PATHWAYS TO RESIDENTIAL INCORPORATION: SOME HYPOTHESES

At least three paths to residential integration can be identified, one for each of the group level theories of residential incorporation presented at the beginning of this chapter. All three of them point to the importance of looking at the effect of ethnic group resources such as size, socioeconomic traits, nativity and length of exposure and cultural norms and values in the kind of integration strategies used by group members. However, the integration of groups is likely to be shaped as much by the setting in which integration takes place as by group factors. Given the discussion on the different contexts and past studies that revealed the group specific nature of integration, three hypotheses by ethnic or racial group can be advanced:

1. White ethnic groups in the U.S. are more likely to follow the path of spatial assimilation than White ethnic groups in Canada.

As White ethnic group members acquire social and economic resources, they would have access to neighborhoods outside of ethnic enclaves and concentrated areas. This is to be expected in both countries due to Whites' privileged positions in both places. However, I hypothesize that we will observe a greater level of residential integration in the United States because the Canadian context supports ethnic retention to a greater degree than the U.S. in terms of its integration policy and ideology.

The association between group resources and residential concentration for these groups is shown graphically in Figure 3.2. The process of spatial assimilation is characterized by a negative association between resources (i.e. socioeconomic and cultural) and residential concentration.

The second hypothesis relates to Black ethnic groups:

> 2.   Black ethnic groups in the U.S. are more likely to follow the path of place stratification than Black ethnic groups in Canada.

The more prominent history of racism and racial residential segregation in the United States suggests that the bipolar model should lead to persistent Black residential segregation in this country compared to Black groups in Canada, where it is less clear whether Blacks are at the bottom of the racial hierarchy. In Figure 3.3, the place stratification perspective is depicted by a flat line, in contrast to the spatial assimilation graph, as it predicts that in spite of increasing resources, residential concentration will not decrease due to the barriers faced by group members in a racialized system.

For Asian ethnic groups, we predict the following:

> 3.   Asian ethnic groups in the U.S. are more likely to follow the path of spatial assimilation than Asian ethnic groups in Canada, where ethnic retention is more likely.

The pressure to assimilate is generally stronger in the United States than in Canada, where the official policy of multiculturalism supports ethnic retention. Given this context, as well as a lack of a clear position for Asian groups in the racial hierarchy of either country, we should expect to find spatial assimilation more likely to operate for Asian groups in the United States but not for comparable groups in Canada. This is akin to the pattern expected for White ethnic groups with some slight differences. The difference lies in the degree to which assimilation is expected. Asian ethnic groups, with increasing resources are expected to move out of concentrated conditions but evidence of residential enclaves for well-resourced group members in the U.S. suggests that the negative slope will be less than for Whites. The ethnic retention argument posits that increasing ethnic group resources can maintain or enhance ethnic group separation and residential distinctiveness, and for Asian groups in Canada, a flat line can be expected in the empirical results (Figure 3.4).

Figure 3.2 Hypothesized group integration in the U.S. and Canada, Whites

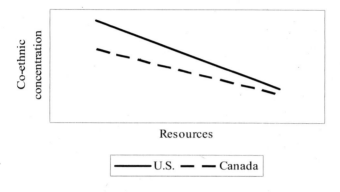

Figure 3.3 Hypothesized group integration in the U.S. and Canada, Blacks

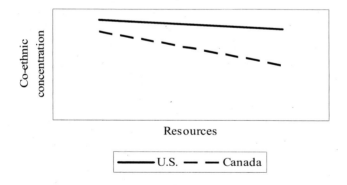

Figure 3.4 Hypothesized group integration in the U.S. and Canada, Asians

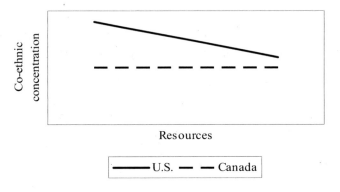

The degree to which a group adheres to hypothesis 1, 2 or 3 will likely also depend on the context of migration and reception arguing for a fourth hypothesis:

4.   Ethnic groups that have a history of migration characterized by primarily economic goals are more likely to follow the path of spatial assimilation than groups that have migrated for primarily other reasons.

The selectivity of economic migrants is likely to result in differences in motivation and orientation compared to refugees. As a group, economic migrants are also likely to have the human capital required for expeditious movement into the economy (Chiswick 1982). Moreover, economic migrants may be more likely to arrive with (or quickly acquire) the understanding that for economic success to occur, they must work outside of the ethnic community (and therefore live outside the ethnic community). In contrast, due to shared experiences of oppression, persecution or catastrophe, involuntary migrants are likely to rely more on ethnic communities and be protective of the group and way of life. Thus, they may be less open to acculturation and integration with members outside the community.

Finally, differences between Canada and the United States suggests that there should be some general cross-national patterns of residential concentration. Namely,

5.   Ethnic and racial groups are less likely to be residentially concentrated in Canada than in the United States.

The less extreme structure of inequality, a more institutionalized settlement sector, and an economically oriented immigration policy (and its impact on migration flows) supports a greater degree of residential dispersion in Canada than in the U.S.

The multiple paths of integration, namely assimilation, stratification and retention and the differences in contexts in which integration occurs suggest that incorporation will be specific to groups and contexts as specified in the hypotheses above. We can directly test whether the spatial assimilation model holds for our ethnic groups with census data but it is difficult to discern between place stratification and ethnic retention in the quantitative analyses. Theoretical expectations along with past studies will help to shed light on the degree to which alternative processes occur for particular groups in Canada and the United States. The data and analyses are presented next.

CHAPTER FOUR

Metropolitan integration:
Data, variables and methods

This chapter describes the data and methods used for the first part of the data analysis. As outlined in the introduction, the analytical strategy is to examine both the general residential patterns of integration across countries by pooling a number of different ethnic groups across many urban areas as well as examining group-specific patterns in particular places. The former strategy will highlight general processes of residential integration for panethnic groups within a national context and permit cross-national comparisons. The latter strategy, described in Chapter Six, will also highlight the processes of residential integration but for specified ethnic groups and is intended to uncover group and local area comparisons, which is limited in the first type of analysis.

This chapter begins with some details of the data and a description of the sample selection process. Then I discuss the operationalization of variables, describe the sample and specify the methods applied.

Data and sample selection

The most recent censuses from the United States and Canada provide data for the analysis. For the U.S., the census was taken in April 2000 and data for the study were obtained from online U.S. census tabulations at the metropolitan, or Metropolitan Statistical Areas/Consolidated Metropolitan Statistical Areas (MSA/CMSA), and census tract levels. Most of the tabulations at the metropolitan level were taken from Summary File 4, which contains social and economic data by ancestry as well as metropolitan area characteristics. Tract level data on ancestry and race groups for the estimation of segregation statistics were obtained from Summary Files 1 and 3.

The Canadian census occurred most recently in May 2001 and tabulations at the metropolitan, or Census Metropolitan Area (CMA), and census tract levels were obtained from Statistics Canada. Canadian data were obtained online as well as through special tabulations. An evaluation of data comparability across the two countries is provided in Appendix A.

This study is concerned with the integration of ethnic groups and immigration history is a relevant feature of this process. This is evidenced by the large foreign-born populations in each country, with 11 percent (or 31,107,889) of the total U.S. population, and 18 percent (or 5,448,480) of the total population of Canada. For group selection purposes, an initial list of the top 25 places of birth for the foreign-born population in each country was derived to ensure that ethnic groupings consisted of substantial numbers of immigrants. From this list, immigrant groups that appeared on both lists were selected, yielding 14 groups (in bold, Table 4.1). Their corresponding ethnic groups, English, German, Italian, Polish, Russian, Iranian, Chinese, Filipino, Vietnamese, Korean, Asian/East Indian, Pakistani, Jamaican and Haitian, are used to compare residential processes across the two countries.

While the definition of ethnic origin or ancestry is likely to be comparable across Canada and the United States (i.e. someone who identifies as Haitian ancestry in the U.S. census is likely to respond similarly in the Canadian census), they vary in the way counts are provided by each of the census offices. For ancestry groups, the U.S. Census Bureau disseminates the tabulations by first and second ancestry separately while Statistics Canada provides numbers by single and multiple origins. For ancestry groups in the U.S. then, the data include counts of those with single *and* multiple origins where the relevant ancestry is a first ancestry.

Due to differences in group migration histories and length of residence in a place – or vintage (White and Glick 1999), ancestry groups in the extracted U.S. dataset vary in their composition of individuals with multiple origins. Greater multiple origin compositions are found in the European ethnic groups, thus the groups that are the least comparable between the two national censuses are the English, German, Italian, Polish and Russian. While multiple origin respondents are also included under Haitian, Jamaican and Iranian, they comprise a very small proportion of each group. This data issue is not relevant for Asian ethnic groups as they fall under the race category and single origin data are available in the U.S. online tabulations. With these ethnic origin and ancestry counts, we observe relatively large numbers of each selected ethnic group in the two countries, with larger populations to be found in the U.S. In fact, all of the ethnic groups included in the sample had more than double the numbers in the U.S. than in Canada (Table 4.2).

For both countries, I concentrate on the residential patterns of the fourteen ethnic groups in all metropolitan areas. There are 27 such areas in Canada and 276 in the U.S. - excluding 4 MSA's in Puerto Rico.[2] These geographic areas provide the most information about ethnic residential integration, as the majority of all ethnic groups are located there (Table 4.2). For all but three groups in Canada (English, German and Russian), more than three quarters of members can be found in metropolitan areas. At this level of geography, the maximum sample size of 3,864 can be obtained for the U.S. sample (14 ethnic groups in 276 metropolitan areas) and 378 for the Canadian one (14 ethnic groups in 27 metropolitan areas).

The small population or non-existence of particular ethnic groups in some areas restricts the sample. Thus, a minimum threshold is applied for inclusion as segregation measures can be sensitive to group sizes and census data are suppressed for very small populations. Various thresholds have been applied elsewhere (Farley and Frey 1996; Langberg and Farley 1985; Massey and Denton 1988). In the sample then, ethnic groups consisting of at least 1,000 members in metropolitan areas are included to maximize the number of ethnic groups and metropolitan areas represented. This translates into 1,718 groups in 275 U.S. metropolitan areas and 189 groups in 25 Canadian metropolitan areas, although not all ethnic groups are present for each metropolitan area counted.

The cross-sectional nature of the data limits our ability to infer long-term processes of residential integration although this is less of a concern when we look at levels of residential concentration. The data only provide a snapshot of underlying processes, but the associations found through the regression analysis may be suggestive of the

---

[2] I exclude metropolitan areas in Puerto Rico due to the different social context, which may affect the results for the U.S. Moreover, a slightly modified census questionnaire is used in that region.

mechanisms that have been specified in the theoretical explanations.

Table 4.1 Top 25 places of birth for the foreign-born

U.S.	Census 2000	Canada	Census 2001
Philippines	1,369,070	**UK**	605,995
China	1,192,437	**China**	568,445
India	1,022,552	**Italy**	315,455
Vietnam	988,174	**India**	314,690
Cuba	872,716	United States	237,920
Korea	864,125	**Philippines**	232,670
Canada	820,771	**Poland**	180,415
El Salvador	817,336	**Germany**	174,070
Germany	706,704	Portugal	153,535
Dominican Republic	687,677	**Viet Nam**	148,405
UK	677,751	Yugoslavia (former)	145,375
Jamaica	553,827	**USSR (former)**	133,200
Colombia	509,872	**Jamaica**	120,210
Guatemala	480,665	Netherlands	117,690
Italy	473,338	Sri Lanka	87,305
Poland	466,742	Guyana	83,535
Haiti	419,317	**Pakistan**	79,310
Japan	347,539	Greece	75,765
Russia	340,177	**Iran**	71,985
Ecuador	298,626	**Korea**	70,635
Iran	283,226	France	69,460
Honduras	282,852	Lebanon	67,225
Peru	278,186	Trinidad and Tobago	64,145
Ukraine	275,153	Romania	60,165
Pakistan	223,477	**Haiti**	52,625

Table 4.2 Selected ethnic group populations

	U.S.	Canada
English	16,627,305	1,479,520
German	30,199,866	705,595
Polish	6,296,538	260,415
Italian	12,906,708	726,275
Russian	1,927,106	70,890
Iranian	317,970	73,450
Chinese[2]	2,314,537	936,210
Indian	1,678,765	581,665
Filipino	1,850,314	266,140
Vietnamese	1,122,528	119,120
Korean	1,076,872	95,200
Pakistani	153,533	54,565
Jamaican	689,001	138,180
Haitian	531,397	70,750

1 First ancestry for English, German, Polish, Italian, Russian, Iranian, Jamaican, Haitian, and race alone for Asian groups (U.S.). Single responses for ethnic origin (Canada).
2. Excludes Taiwanese.

Table 4.3 Selected ethnic group populations in metropolitan areas

	U.S.	Percent	Canada	Percent
English	12,900,000	78	857,070	58
German	23,000,000	76	360,020	51
Polish	5,580,309	89	213,625	82
Italian	11,800,000	91	660,740	91
Russian	1,826,126	95	50,350	71
Iranian	312,336	98	71,775	98
Chinese[2]	2,262,587	98	907,405	97
Indian	1,628,855	97	552,180	95
Filipino	1,750,084	95	254,925	96
Vietnamese	1,098,024	98	111,395	94
Korean	1,036,341	96	89,475	94
Pakistani	150,162	98	53,150	97
Jamaican	677,073	98	135,225	98
Haitian	525,194	99	68,985	98

Dependent variable

Ethnic residential integration

In the context of an immigrant society, integration can occur in a minimum of four different directions (Breton 1964). The mainstream community is the direction that is often implied by the concept of integration. However, immigrants can also integrate into the co-ethnic community, a different ethnic community or no community (i.e. anomie). Furthermore, the integration process is not mutually exclusive and most immigrants are likely to integrate into more than one of these cultural groups. Along any single dimension then, ethnic group members may be more or less integrated with a particular community (Breton et al. 1990). In this study on residential patterns, integration is defined as any community other than the co-ethnic community. For example, for White ethnic group members, this can include residential proximity to other White ethnic groups, Black or Asian ethnic groups. Thus, distinctive ethnic residential patterns would suggest that ethnic groups are more likely to be neighbors with one another than with those outside of the co-ethnic community.

I move away from the Anglo-conformity model that characterizes many other studies of residential assimilation. Assimilation does not necessarily imply one direction (Gordon 1964; Alba and Nee 1997). I also distance this analysis from the question of segmented assimilation. The question of the neighborhood composition for those ethnic group members who residentially disperse is an important question, but not one to be investigated here. Rather, this study aims to identify the processes by which ethnic groups become less residentially distinctive *as a group* and to explore whether the salience of ethnicity as an organizing principle of urban space varies across contexts.

Following the work of Massey and colleagues (1988; 1996) and of Johnston, Poulsen and Forrest (2007a) to some extent, who found segregation to be multidimensional, three segregation indices – the index of dissimilarity, the entropy index and the isolation index – are estimated for each ethnic group in each metropolitan area using census tract tabulations. The first two provide a measure of evenness, which refers to the differential distribution of a group and the third is a measure of potential interaction or contact.

The index of dissimilarity is used most often in the two-group case, where values are interpreted as the proportion of a group that must be redistributed in order to obtain the same geographic distribution as the reference group. This index is commonly applied to studies of residential segregation and has now become the true "workhorse" of segregation indices, especially in the literature on ethnic and racial residential segregation (White 1986). From the classic to more recent studies that compared racial and ethnic group segregation across a number of cities (Frey and Farley 1996; Lieberson 1963; Massey and Denton 1987; Taeuber and Taeuber 1965) and for studies of groups in one place (a selection of studies includes Chicago (Taeuber and Taeuber 1964), Detroit (Darden and Kamel 2000), New Jersey (White and Omer 1997) and New York City (Kantrowitz 1973), this index of segregation seems to be the preferred statistic. Its frequent application can be attributed to its user-friendly characteristics in computation and interpretation, its high correlation with other indices and its established history (Massey and Denton 1988; Massey, White and Phua 1996).

Also known as the information theory index (Theil and Finizza 1971), the entropy index offers a measure of the percentage reduction of error (White 1986). In other words, it provides an indication of how well one could predict the ethnic identity of a person by knowing where they live. The entropy index is the weighted average deviation of each neighborhood's diversity from the metropolitan-level diversity, standardized by the metropolitan-level diversity. The entropy index is valued for its decomposition properties as well as for its ability to handle multiple group situations. It can also be used, as it is in this study, with two groups.

The isolation index, a measure of residential exposure, captures the probability that two randomly selected people sharing the same neighborhood will be from the same ethnic group. It refers to the degree of isolation experienced by members of a group in the metropolitan area as it takes into account the group population, leading some to prefer this measure over evenness measures (Lieberson 1980). The isolation value gives the ethnic group proportion of a neighborhood for the average group member. This index is also commonly applied in studies of residential segregation.

The mathematical operations of each segregation measure are specified as follows:

For the **Dissimilarity Index**:

$$D = \frac{1}{2}\left|\sum_{i=1}^{I} \frac{n_1}{N_1} - \frac{n_2}{N_2}\right|$$

where n_1 is size of group 1 in tract i;

n_2 is size of all others in tract i;

N_1 is total size of group 1 in the metropolitan area;

N_2 is total size of all others in the metropolitan area.

For the **Entropy Index**:

$$E = \sum_{i=1}^{I} \frac{n_i (E^* - \overline{E})}{NE^*}$$

$$E^* = (P_g * \ln(\frac{1}{P_g})) + ((1 - P_g) * \ln(\frac{1}{1 - P_g}))$$

$$\overline{E} = (p_{gi} * \ln(\frac{1}{p_{gi}})) + ((1 - p_{gi}) * \ln(\frac{1}{1 - p_{gi}}))$$

where p_{gi} is the proportion of group g in tract i;
        P_g is the proportion of group g in the metropolitan area;
        n_i is size of tract i;
        N is the total size of the metropolitan area.

For the **Isolation Index**:

$$_xP_x^* = \sum_{i=1}^{I} ((\frac{n_1}{N_1}) * (\frac{n_1}{n_i}))$$

where n_1 is size of group 1 in tract i;
        n_i is size of tract i;
        N_1 is total size of group 1 in the metropolitan area.

All indices are bounded between 0 and 1 with lower values indicating higher levels of integration, or less distinctive residential patterns. Non-group members are the reference category for the Dissimilarity and Entropy indices. Census tract data of the fourteen ethnic groups in both countries are used to estimate the above three segregation values. As found elsewhere (Massey et al. 1988; 1996;

White, Kim and Glick 2005), the Entropy Index is highly correlated with the Dissimilarity Index giving a Pearson correlation coefficient of .95 and resulting in duplicate analyses if both indices are used. The Isolation Index shows a correlation of r=-.42 and -.29 with the Dissimilarity and Entropy Indices respectively.

For the analysis, I focus on the Dissimilarity and Isolation indices for several reasons. Both indices are frequently applied in the segregation literature and they each have the advantage of having a more straightforward interpretation. Moreover, they measure two different dimensions of segregation allowing us to identify how residential processes might differ according to the dimension of residential segregation. Analysis of the Dissimilarity Index will show how group factors affect the spread of ethnic groups across urban neighborhoods within metropolitan areas. Analysis of the Isolation Index will reveal to what extent various group factors are associated with potential physical contact and intergroup exposure.

In the statistical analysis, the logit values of these two indices are applied due to their bounded nature and to ensure that predicted segregation statistics fall within the range 0 to 1. The logit transformation follows this equation:

$$l(p) = \ln(\frac{p}{1-p})$$

And the conversion of the logits back to their original scales is given by:

$$p = (\frac{1}{1 + \exp^{(-1*l(p))}})$$

Pooling all metropolitan area ethnic groups in the sample by country, the mean value of the logit for the Dissimilarity and Isolation indices for the U.S. sample is $-.76$ and -3.4, respectively (or .32 and .03 in their original scales). For the Canadian sample, mean values are $-.4$ and -3.52, respectively (or .4 and .03 in their original scales). Overall, there is little difference in the mean segregation levels between the two samples although the Canadian sample is slightly more segregated. A closer examination of ethnic differences across countries is provided in Chapter Five.

Explanatory variables

Ethnic resources

The key explanatory concept includes both what is referred to in the ethnic economies literature as ethnic resources and class resources. The former refers to the social features that are particular to an ethnic group and includes the values, attitudes, solidarity and institutions while the concept of class resources refers to both cultural and material resources and includes human capital and economic class values (Light and Bonacich 1988; Light and Gold 2000). Together, these concepts identify the importance of cultural, political, social and economic capital among community members for distinctive patterns of integration. Whereas Light and Bonacich (1988) distinguish between the two types of resources, I use the term as an umbrella label to identify the ethnic basis of those resources while recognizing the multidimensional nature of this concept.

This multidimensional view of ethnic resources coupled with the availability of numerous indicators in the data permit the application of a data reduction technique, in particular, principal components analysis. The advantage of this technique lies in its ability to linearize an assortment of variables into a few key factors taking into account correlations between variables. Where there are multiple indicators that are highly correlated and that potentially reflect the same underlying concept, it is an appropriate method for dealing with problems of collinearity in the model. Moreover, it allows for the inclusion of multiple indicators into an index rather than limiting the researcher to the selection of one or two variables.

Ethnic resource variables are measured at the metropolitan level for each ethnic group included in the sample and they include indicators of composition, life cycle stage, socioeconomic status and acculturation. Initially, eleven continuous variables from all available observations in the U.S. and Canadian samples were pooled and then entered into the procedure using Stata 7.0 (n=2,496). Four variables, group size, proportion self-employed, proportion female and proportion married, did not appear to be highly correlated with the others and were removed from the procedure.

The remaining seven indicators are include the proportion of older adults, proportion foreign-born, proportion speaking no official language(s), proportion of newcomers, proportion with a university degree, median male income (in U.S.$) and proportion unemployed. Details on their operationalization are provided in Table 4.4. Table 4.5 provides the results of the principal components analysis using these seven variables and a varimax (or orthogonal) rotation.[3] Using the Kaiser criterion (Eigenvalues greater than 1.0), two factors are selected and together, they extract approximately 60 per cent of the variance.

Based on the scoring coefficients, the two factors can be labelled acculturation and socioeconomic status. The three variables with higher scores on the first factor are proportion older adults, proportion foreign-born and proportion speaking no official language(s). Ethnic groups scoring high on this factor are less likely to be acculturated as they are likely to have a younger age structure, be more immigrant and have lower levels of official language acquisition. For ease of interpretation these scores have been inverted such that higher scores signify higher levels of acculturation. The mean score on acculturation for the U.S. sample is .19 and -.14 for the sample in Canada (Table 4.7). This should be expected given the greater share of immigrants in Canada's population as compared with the United States.

The second factor weighs more heavily on socioeconomic indicators such as the median income of males,[4] proportion of individuals with a university degree, and the unemployment rate. A fourth indicator, that of proportion newcomers, is also a stronger indicator of SES than it is of acculturation. Given that newcomers are still settling into the economic system and are likely to fall towards the lower end of the occupational ladder, we might argue that ethnic groups with higher proportions of newcomers are also likely to be those with lower levels of SES. And there is evidence to suggest that recent cohorts of immigrants compared to earlier waves are faring worse on earnings (Picot, Hou and Coulombe 2008).

In the data examined here, the Canadian sample, on average, falls below the U.S. sample on the SES factor score with -.64. The U.S. score is .002 (Table 4.7).

---

[3] An oblique rotation using promax(3) showed a very low correlation between factors (r=.0001).
[4] For groups in Canada, income was converted to U.S. dollars using the 2001 annual average exchange rate from the Bank of Canada.

Table 4.4 Indicators of ethnic resources

Variables	U.S.
Older adults	Proportion 65+ years
Foreign-born	Proportion foreign-born
No official language(s)	Proportion with ability to speak English "not well" or "not at all", 5+ yrs
Newcomers	Proportion foreign-born arrived in previous 5 year period
Education	Proportion with university degree Bachelor's and above
Income	Median, males 15+ yrs with income in $1,000's
Unemployment	Proportion unemployed, 16+ yrs in labour force

Variables	Canada
Older adults	Proportion 65+ years
Foreign-born	Proportion immigrant and nonpermanent residents
No official language(s)	Proportion with no knowledge of official languages
Newcomers	Proportion foreign-born arrived in previous 5 year period
Education	Proportion with university degree Bachelor's and above
Income	Median, males 15+ yrs with income in $1,000's Converted to U.S.$ using 2001 average exchange rate (1.55)
Unemployment	Proportion unemployed, 15+ yrs in labour force

Table 4.5 Principal components analysis on ethnic resources

Factor	Eigenvalue	Difference	Proportion	Cumulative
1	2.493	0.818	0.36	0.36
2	1.675	0.792	0.24	0.6

Varimax rotated factor loadings

Variable	1. Acculturation	2. SES	Uniqueness
Older adults	-0.68	-0.13	0.52
Foreign-born	0.86	0.14	0.24
No official language(s)	0.78	-0.06	0.39
Newcomers	0.44	0.54	0.52
Education	0.23	0.85	0.22
Income	-0.48	0.67	0.33
Unemployment	0.45	-0.43	0.62

Scoring coefficients

Variable	1. Acculturation[*]	2. SES
Older adults	-0.27	-0.07
Foreign-born	0.34	0.06
No official language(s)	0.31	-0.05
Newcomers	0.17	0.31
Education	0.08	0.5
Income	-0.21	0.41
Unemployment	0.19	-0.27

n=2,496

[*] For ease of interpretation this factor is multiplied by -1 in the analysis.

All ethnic resource variables are measured at the aggregate level, for ethnic groups in metropolitan areas. The model then provides a test of which resources at a group level are associated with residential integration. The results of this ecological model preclude making inferences regarding the individual behavior of group members but allow us to observe the effect of differences in group level factors.

On theoretical and methodological grounds, group size and proportion self-employed remain included in the models as separate variables (Table 4.6). Group size acts as a resource for members such that larger groups not only have greater visibility and presence but also have a population base for accessing other kinds of resources and services. The population size of an ethnic group has also been known to influence residential segregation statistics, generally in a negative direction. The natural log of group size is used in the multivariate models and the descriptive statistics in Table 4.7 show that U.S. ethnic groups are generally larger than comparable groups in Canada.

The self-employment rate could also have a unique association with residential patterns although this is often perceived to be an effect of residential concentration and not a determinant (Waldinger, McEvoy and Aldrich 1990). Nevertheless, as a potential source of social mobility, its effect on residential patterns may be an important aspect of ethnic integration. On this trait, ethnic groups in Canada tend to have higher rates of self-employment than groups in the U.S. (Table 4.7).

Urban and regional context

The urban ecological framework argues that the urban setting plays a role in shaping population distribution (Farley and Frey 1994; Fong 1996; Park, Burgess and McKenzie 1925; Massey and Denton 1987). Over time, urban areas develop in unique ways, shaped by individuals as well as shaping individuals' social, economic and spatial organization. Factors such as local governance structures and the allocation of resources, housing markets, the size and demographic composition of the area including the presence of other ethnic groups, the economic base or functional specialization and the history of immigration all appear to have an impact on residential processes and settlement patterns.

With the data available, the urban context is measured by four indicators at the metropolitan area level: population size (logged), proportion of new housing construction in the decade prior to the census, proportion of owner-occupied homes, and industry base (Table 3.5).[5] Previous studies of U.S. metropolitan segregation have classified metropolitan areas according to their functional specialization such as durable manufacturing, non-durable manufacturing, retirement, university, government and military (Farley and Frey 1994). Since Canadian metropolitan areas are less amenable to this type of classification, mostly due to data limitations and the small number of metropolitan areas, I use industry base instead. I first generate standardized scores for the percentage employed in each industry in each metropolitan area by country and then identify those industries that fall above the mean and sum across them. This ordinal variable measures how many industries employ a large share of the population and provides an indication of the diversification of the industrial base for a given metropolitan area.

Descriptive statistics in Table 4.7 show that for those ethnic groups included in the sample, metropolitan areas are generally larger in the U.S. than in Canada, that levels of homeownership are comparable although slightly higher in the U.S., that the U.S. has a greater share of new housing construction. In terms of the industrial base, more than one third of the U.S. sample have only 1 large industry whereas more than one third of the Canadian sample have 2 large industries.[6]

In addition to unique urban environments, regional variations across Canada and the United States suggest that this may be an important aspect to control. Four regions are listed for the U.S. and four for Canada. These are listed in Table 4.6. The U.S. sample is comprised of largely southern metropolitan areas and the Canadian sample weighs heavily on those places in Ontario and the west (Table 4.7).

---

[5] The per cent foreign-born and non-white were omitted from the analysis due to multicollinearity. Both variables have a significant, positive effect on segregation in the bivariate analysis (with the exception of Isolation in the U.S. sample) but with the inclusion of metropolitan population size in the multivariate model, they lose their predictive power.

[6] Bear in mind that metropolitan areas may be represented more than once in these descriptive statistics.

Panethnicity/racial grouping

The development of panethnic and racial labels reflects a shift in ethnic group identities to a broader level (Espiritu 1992). This occurs through a process of racialization where a collectivity of national origin or ancestry groups are perceived to share similar features such as language or phenotype and ethnic groups have been shown to cluster according to panethnic groupings (Kim and White 2004). The place stratification hypothesis provides a further argument for the importance of this variable in explaining residential patterns and suggests that residential processes vary by panethnicity/race making it a key interacting variable. In the models, I interact panethnicity/race with the two extracted ethnic resource factors, acculturation and socioeconomic status. In the pooled model, this is also interacted with the country variable as levels of residential segregation are expected to vary according to panethnicity/race across the two countries.

The sample is allocated into one of three panethnic/racial groups, White, Black or Asian and the coding of ethnic groups is provided in Table 4.6.[7] As Table 4.7 shows, White ethnic groups comprise the majority followed by Asian ethnic groups and Black ethnic groups in both samples.

National context

Direct measures of each of the five dimensions discussed in Chapter Two are not available. However, we do expect to find cross-country differences in levels of residential concentration as exposited in the hypotheses and I include a dummy variable for Canada in the pooled analysis.

---

[7] Latinos are excluded from this analysis as there were no groups from Latin America in the Canadian census data that were of sufficient population size to be included and compared with the United States.

Table 4.6 Measurement of explanatory variables

Variables	U.S.	Canada
Ethnic Group Characteristics		
Group size	First ancestry/Asian alone	Single ethnic origin
	Natural log	Natural log
Self-employment	Proportion self-employed, 16+ yrs in labour force	Proportion self-employed, 15+ yrs in labour force
Acculturation	See Table 3.4	See Table 3.4
Socioeconomic status	See Table 3.4	See Table 3.4
Panethnicity		
White	English, German, Italian, Polish, Russian, Iranian = 1; 0 otherwise	
Black	Jamaican, Haitian = 1; 0 otherwise	
Asian	Indian, Pakistani, Chinese, Vietnamese, Korean, Filipino = 1; 0 otherwise	
Metropolitan Context		
Population size	Natural log	Natural log
New housing construction	Proportion of homes constructed from 1995 to 2000	Proportion of homes constructed from 1996 to 2001
Home ownership	Proportion owner-occupied homes	Proportion owner-occupied homes

cont'd next page

Table 4.6 (cont'd) Measurement of explanatory variables

cont'd from previous page

Variables	U.S.	Canada

Metropolitan Context (cont'd)

Industry base   Dummy variable if greater than 1 standard deviation above mean for all metro areas, then summed across industries:

0 = If metro area is not above 1 standard deviation for any industry

1 = If metro area is above 1 standard deviation in 1 industry

2 = If metro area is above 1 standard deviation in each of 2 industries

3 = If metro area is above 1 standard deviation in each of 3 or more industries

Region

U.S.	Canada
West	Ontario
Midwest	Québec
Northeast	West
South	East

Table 4.7 Descriptive statistics for multivariate analysis, means and proportions

Variables	U.S.	Canada
	mean/pr.(std.dev.)	*mean/pr.(std.dev.)*
Dependent variables		
Dissimilarity index (logit)	-.76 (-0.8)	-.40 (-0.9)
Isolation index (logit)	-3.40 (-1.2)	-3.52 (-1.0)
Ethnic resources		
Acculturation (factor score)	.19 (-1.0)	-.14 (-1.2)
Socioeconomic status (factor score)	.00 (-0.9)	-.64 (-0.7)
Group size (logged)	9.10 (-1.5)	8.90 (-1.4)
Self-employment	.10 (-0.04)	.12 (-0.07)
Panethnicity		
White	.69 (-0.5)	.52 (-0.5)
Black	.04 (-0.2)	.07 (-0.3)
Asian	.28 (-0.4)	.41 (-0.5)
Metropolitan context		
Population size (logged)	14.40 (-27.9)	11.40 (-12.9)
Home ownership	.66 (-0.06)	.65 (-0.06)
New housing	.10 (-0.05)	.07 (-0.03)
Metropolitan context (cont'd)		
Industry (3 or more)	.25 (-0.4)	.32 (-0.5)
0	.11 (-0.3)	--
1	.36 (-0.5)	.30 (-0.5)
2	.28 (-0.5)	.38 (-0.5)

cont'd next page

Table 4.7 (cont'd) Descriptive statistics for multivariate analysis, means and proportions

cont'd from previous page

Variables	U.S.	Canada
	mean/pr.(std.dev.)	*mean/pr.(std.dev.)*
U.S. Regions		
West	.21 (-0.4)	n/a
Mid-west	.24 (-0.4)	n/a
North-east	.15 (-0.4)	n/a
South	.41 (-0.5)	n/a
Regions in Canada		
Ontario	n/a	.49 (-0.5)
Québec	n/a	.10 (-0.3)
BC & Prairies	n/a	.37 (-0.5)
Maritimes	n/a	.04 (-0.2)
N	1,718	189

Analytical methods

Using the aggregate data described in Table 4.7, I employ OLS multivariate regression of ethnic residential integration, separately for the Dissimilarity and Isolation indices, on the interaction of ethnic resources and panethnic/racial grouping controlling for the urban context and region for each of the two countries. The model specification for the Dissimilarity Index is as follows:

$$l(\hat{D}) = a + \sum_{i=1}^{4} b_i X_i + \sum_{j=1}^{2} b_j X_j + \sum_{i=1}^{2}\sum_{j=1}^{2} b_k X_i X_j + \sum b_l X_l + \sum b_m X_m$$

The predicted value of Dissimilarity (logit) in a metropolitan area ($l(\hat{D})$) is a linear function of ethnic group resources (X_i, where X_{i1} and X_{i2} are acculturation and SES respectively), panethnic or racial grouping (X_j, where X_{j1} and X_{j2} are Black and Asian respectively), metropolitan area characteristics (X_l), and a dummy-coded region variable (X_m). The same model is applied to the predicted value of Isolation ($l(\hat{I})$).

A final, pooled model adds the country dummy (X_n) interacted with panethnicity/race (X_j):

$$l(\hat{D})=a+\sum_{i=1}^{4}b_iX_i+\sum_{j=1}^{2}b_jX_j+\sum_{i=1}^{2}\sum_{j=1}^{2}b_kX_iX_j+\sum b_lX_l+\sum b_mX_m+b_nX_n+\sum_{j=1}^{2}b_pX_jX_n$$

A methodological implication raised by this data analysis method is the ecological fallacy. The ecological model permits the examination of aggregate processes but limits inferences about individual behavior (Robinson 1950). That is, segregation statistics using census tract data for a city does not tell us about patterns within census tracts (Lieberson 1963). An inferential error is made when individual behavior is assumed to correspond to aggregate behavior (Alba and Logan 1993). Furthermore, associations found among the variables in the model at the metropolitan level may not apply at the neighborhood or individual level. In this study then, a link between an ethnic group's socioeconomic resources and residential segregation levels at the metropolitan level cannot be generalized to the level of the neighborhood or individual, although some suggest that the patterns are not completely inconsistent (Massey and Denton 1985). In general, we cannot extrapolate our interpretations beyond or interpolate within the boundaries of the scale of analysis. The results of statistical tests, presented in the next chapter, can only be generalized to the level of the ethnic group and to behavior at the metropolitan level.

CHAPTER FIVE

Panethnicity and ethnic resources in metropolitan residential integration

This chapter reviews the empirical results of the data analysis procedure outlined in Chapter Four. In doing so, it seeks to shed light on ethnic residential integration in two host societies, Canada and the United States. Two key questions are addressed in this chapter: Are there cross-national differences in the levels and processes of ethnic residential integration? And, what is the effect of panethnicity or race in this cross-national perspective?

The findings discussed here will inform our understanding of integration processes at the metropolitan level and of the context-specific nature of immigrant and ethnic adaptation. The degree to which ethnic groups follow the paths of assimilation, stratification or retention in their adjustment to host societies may be explained by the setting in which settlement takes place, in addition to group factors. One aspect of host societies in particular, the panethnic and racial structure, is not only expected to shape intergroup relations but also to affect the process of integration itself. To address this empirically, I test the interacting effect of panethnic or racial grouping and ethnic resources on ethnic residential patterns.

In the first section, the levels of ethnic segregation observed in metropolitan areas within each of the two countries are described. Then I examine the effect of ethnic resources on metropolitan residential segregation controlling for the urban context and regional location, and compare results across the two host societies. This analysis does not focus on the individual paths of particular ethnic groups but rather, on the general processes of ethnic residential integration and patterns by panethnicity or race across metropolitan areas. The degree to which the explanatory variables account for panethnic differences between countries is addressed in the last section. A more focused analysis on

69

particular ethnic groups at the neighborhood level is offered in Chapters Six and Seven.

LEVELS OF ETHNIC RESIDENTIAL SEGREGATION IN METROPOLITAN AREAS

There is ethnic variation in the level of segregation in Canada and the United States as well as some variation across the two countries and these patterns are affected by the choice of index. Tables 5.1 and 5.2 lists the mean values of the two segregation indices applied in this study, the Dissimilarity Index and the Isolation Index, for each of the 14 ethnic groups in the U.S. and Canadian samples. The number of metropolitan areas represented for each ethnic group is also provided in the table. Graphs for each of the two segregation indices are presented in Figures 5.1 and 5.2.

European ethnic groups, overall, appear to be the most evenly distributed across neighborhoods in the urban areas of both places (as indicated by the Dissimilarity Index) yet they are also the most isolated, as they are more likely than other groups to come across a neighbor with the same ethnic background. This pattern is the most extreme in the German case. Moreover, in addition to their generally lower levels of uneven population distribution, more than 200 metropolitan areas in the U.S. have greater than 1,000 members of each European group, with the exception of Russians who are represented in a fewer number of areas, and are also more segregated than the other European groups in both countries. The higher levels of segregation of Russians may be explained by the subpopulation of Russian Jews, who for religious reasons, tend to congregate spatially (Peach 2005).

This pattern is evident in Canada as well (although at a much lower scale), with the majority of metropolitan areas in Canada represented for the four European groups. Of the five groups, Russians are counted in the fewest number of metropolitan areas.

In contrast to European ethnic groups, Iranians, considered to be members of a white ethnic group in the U.S. census (and are counted as White in this analysis), are among the most highly segregated in both countries in terms of the Dissimilarity Index yet scored low on the Isolation Index. This is not surprising given the sensitivity of these indices to small group sizes. These mean values are based on the 30 metropolitan areas in the U.S. and the 6 in Canada that meet the threshold for inclusion.

Along with Iranians, the two Caribbean ethnic groups are the most highly segregated in the U.S. sample according to the Dissimilarity Index but they are less segregated than Iranians and several Asian ethnic groups in Canada. This finding, that Blacks are more segregated than Asians in the U.S. but not in Canada, is consistent with the pattern found by others (Fong 1996; Johnston et al. 2007a; Peach 2005). Of the two Caribbean groups in the sample, Haitians are more isolated than Jamaicans and this is evident in the metropolitan areas of both countries, which, for this panethnic group, is small in number (U.S. n=63; Canada n=13). Haitians are represented in only 2 metropolitan areas in Canada and the small sample sizes are taken into consideration in the regression analysis.

Moderate to high levels on the Dissimilarity Index are found for Asian subgroups, and in general, they are higher than that found for Europeans in both countries. No clear panethnic pattern emerges in the Isolation Index. There is, however, some degree of variation across Asian ethnic groups, with a similar point difference in Dissimilarity (.23-.24) between the most segregated Asian ethnic group and the least, within a country. The difference in Isolation is larger in Canada than in the U.S. (.05 vs. .02). The statistics also show that the most integrated Asian subgroups in the U.S. are not the same as in Canada. Filipinos are the most evenly distributed Asian subgroup in U.S. metropolitan neighborhoods and are also low on the Isolation Index. In Canada, the Chinese have the lowest Dissimilarity value yet one of the highest Isolation scores. Again, this is not surprising given the sensitivity of the Isolation Index to group sizes.

Based on the evenness measure, segregation levels across countries are similar for several groups, ranging from .20 for the English to .50 for Asian/East Indians in both places. However, for four Asian groups, Filipinos, Vietnamese, Koreans and Pakistanis, and for two European groups, Germans and Italians, segregation in Canada is at a much higher level than in the U.S. The largest gaps can be found for Italians, Filipinos and Koreans. These groups are approximately .12 to .15 points more segregated in Canada than in the U.S.

The gap lies in the opposite direction for Iranians, Jamaicans and Haitians. Their levels of segregation are significantly higher in the United States compared to Canada, with values falling between .68 and

.75 in the U.S. and .54 to .63 in Canada. About two thirds of each of these groups would have to move neighborhoods in order to have the same distribution as the remainder of the population.

Table 5.1 Mean ethnic segregation indices, U.S.

Groups	# of metros	D (min, max)		$_xP_x$ (min, max)	
English	275	**.20**	(.09, .47)	**.08**	(.02, .28)
German	275	**.18**	(.06, .43)	**.15**	(.03, .53)
Italian	264	**.25**	(.09, .51)	**.05**	(.008, .24)
Polish	219	**.28**	(.11, .56)	**.03**	(.006, .22)
Russian	117	**.45**	(.26, .67)	**.02**	(.005, .09)
Iranian	30	**.75**	(.57, .9)	**.01**	(.004, .06)
Jamaican	44	**.68**	(.46, .85)	**.02**	(.004, .12)
Haitian	19	**.75**	(.56, .94)	**.05**	(.005, .2)
Chinese	102	**.48**	(.31, .62)	**.03**	(.004, .2)
Indian	108	**.49**	(.31, .64)	**.02**	(.004, .16)
Filipino	80	**.39**	(.24, .62)	**.02**	(.002, .32)
Vietnamese	84	**.55**	(.42, .71)	**.03**	(.003, .16)
Korean	84	**.46**	(.27, .61)	**.02**	(.003, .11)
Pakistani	17	**.63**	(.54, .72)	**.007**	(.002, .02)
mean (min, max)	1,718	.34	(.06, .94)	.06	(.002, .53)

Table 5.2 Mean ethnic segregation indices, Canada

Groups	# of metros	D (min, max)		$_xP_x$ (min, max)	
English	25	**.19**	(.09, .56)	**.07**	(.004, .21)
German	22	**.22**	(.12, .52)	**.04**	(.005, .10)
Italian	19	**.37**	(.26, .55)	**.06**	(.004, .23)
Polish	18	**.30**	(.19, .5)	**.02**	(.009, .05)
Russian	8	**.48**	(.31-.69)	**.01**	(.004, .03)
Iranian	6	**.63**	(.57, .73)	**.02**	(.007, .05)
Jamaican	11	**.54**	(.39, .75)	**.01**	(.004, .05)
Haitian	2	**.57**	(.57, .57)	**.05**	(.02, .08)
Chinese	20	**.46**	(.34, .64)	**.07**	(.007, .32)
Indian	17	**.50**	(.4, .67)	**.07**	(.01, .26)
Filipino	13	**.51**	(.38, .76)	**.04**	(.008, .18)
Vietnamese	11	**.61**	(.47, .75)	**.03**	(.02, .04)
Korean	9	**.61**	(.45, .83)	**.02**	(.006, .04)
Pakistani	8	**.69**	(.55, .82)	**.02**	(.009, .03)
mean (min, max)	189	.42	(.09, .83)	.04	(.004, .32)

Figure 5.1 Mean Dissimilarity Index by group

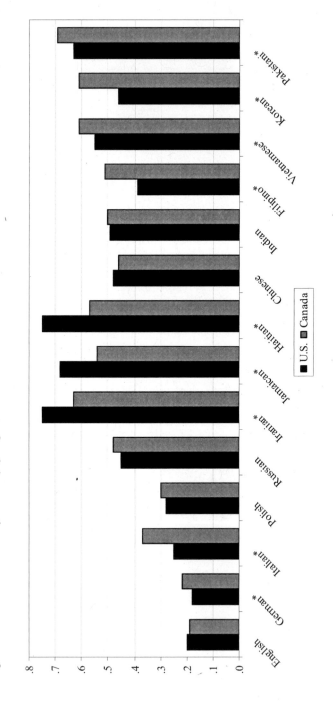

* Statistically significant differences between U.S. and Canada (p<.05).

Figure 5.2 Mean Isolation Index by group

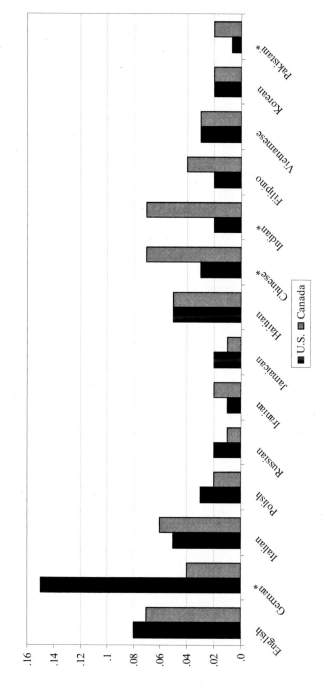

* Statistically significant differences between U.S. and Canada (p<.05).

The Isolation Index measures the probability of group members sharing a neighborhood. Whereas the Dissimilarity Index is a measure of evenness or population distribution across neighborhoods, the Isolation Index provides some indication of the potential contact or interaction between co-ethnic members in the metropolitan area. For most of the groups in the sample, the degree of isolation is similar across countries. However, four ethnic groups faced significantly different degrees of isolation in the two different places. For three of these groups, Chinese, Asian/East Indians and Pakistanis, isolation was greater in Canada than in the United States. Germans faced higher isolation in the U.S. compared to Canada. The higher Isolation and Dissimilarity levels for Haitians suggest that this group is one of the most residentially distinctive groups, especially in the United States but also in Canada.

These segregation statistics underscore two points. First, when we speak of residential segregation, we need to specify which dimension is being measured. The two segregation indices show that groups highly segregated on one index may be low on another.[8] These indices are capturing different dimensions of segregation and it would seem appropriate to keep them separate. These results also reinforce the importance of examining different indices as segregation is a multidimensional concept (Johnston et al. 2007a; Massey and Denton 1988; Massey, White and Phua 1996). I keep the indices separate in the multivariate analysis in order to explore how group factors might affect each dimension and whether there may be differences in the processes that determine unevenness and isolation. It will be interesting to observe to what extent similar results are obtained in the effects of our explanatory variables across the two indices, as that will indicate whether the determinants of segregation are common across dimensions. Second, segregation levels vary by ethnic group and by country. This suggests that both group-related factors and contextual factors are relevant to explaining residential outcomes. I consider this in the next section, which discusses the results of statistical tests.

---

[8] The Pearson correlation coefficient for the Dissimilarity and Isolation Indices is -.14 for the Canadian sample and -.46 for the U.S.

EXPLAINING RESIDENTIAL SEGREGATION

The effect of ethnic resources

The spatial assimilation perspective highlights two factors, socioeconomic status and acculturation, to describe the process of residential integration. Clear evidence of this process, according to this perspective, would be supported by a negative association between each of these two factors and residential segregation. For ethnic retention to be a plausible explanation, the acculturation dimension should not be associated with decreasing segregation rates. Accordingly, for place stratification to be operating, we should observe no association between socioeconomic status and residential distinctiveness. However, it must be stated that the presence of these associations does not prove the existence of either of the latter two processes but some interpretations can be offered based on our current state of knowledge regarding these groups. We also work with the limitation that our data are cross-sectional; we cannot observe changes over time. In other words, we cannot ascertain how increasing acculturation or SES for a given individual over time is associated with residential mobility.

Tables 5.3 to 5.7 present the unstandardized coefficients from three regression models using the logit transformation of the two segregation indices as dependent variables, $l(D)$ for the logit of the Dissimilarity Index and $l(_xP_x)$ for the logit of the Isolation Index, for each country separately. The degree of residential segregation is regressed on the explanatory variables including an interaction model that tests whether the effects of the two ethnic resource variables, acculturation and socioeconomic status, vary by panethnicity or race.

First, looking at the results using the logit of the Dissimilarity Index, column $l(D)$ in Model I, Table 5.3, we see that acculturation is negatively associated with residential segregation in the United States, controlling for other ethnic resources, and this is statistically significant ($p<.05$).[9] As

---

[9] P values were set to .05 and .1 throughout the analysis due to the relatively small number of cases for several of the models. I keep in mind that these thresholds may result in an increase in the study-wise error rate as opposed to more stringent thresholds (i.e. the potential to find statistical significance increases positively with the number of statistical tests) and that the potential for Type I error could be reduced. However,

expected, ethnic groups become more residentially integrated in metropolitan areas as they become more acculturated (i.e. in terms of nativity, language acquisition and age structure, see Chapter Four for a description of the principal components results), net of socioeconomic status scores, group size and proportion self-employed. The same effect of acculturation on the Dissimilarity logit is observed in the Canadian sample (column $l(D)$ in Model I, Table 5.4). However, when we turn to Isolation (column $l(_xP_x)$ in Model I, Tables 5.3 and 5.4), acculturation appears to have a positive effect although this is statistically significant only in the U.S. case.

Still focusing on the results in Model I, we can see that the effect of socioeconomic status on Dissimilarity differs across the two countries. In the U.S. context, this variable shows a statistically significant positive effect on segregation, net of other ethnic resources. In Canada, there appears to be no statistically significant effect ($p<.1$). For both countries, higher socioeconomic status scores are associated with lower levels of Isolation, net of controls.

For both countries, group size has a significant negative effect on residential evenness (column $l(D)$ in Model I, Tables 5.3 and 5.4) net of covariates and the opposite effect on residential isolation (column $l(_xP_x)$ in Model I, Tables 5.3 and 5.4). This should be expected as group sizes influence these measurements. In terms of the Dissimilarity Index, which measures the spread of ethnic groups in neighborhoods, larger groups are likely to have members in more neighborhoods leading to generally lower values and smaller groups are likely to be contained in fewer neighborhoods thereby increasing Dissimilarity statistics. The latter index, a measure of interaction, is also sensitive to group size. That is, the probability of interacting with your own group is higher when there are more members of your group available.

Net of group size, acculturation and socioeconomic status, the effect of proportion self-employed in the ethnic group has a positive effect on Dissimilarity but reduces Isolation in U.S. metropolitan areas. This final variable in Model I shows no statistically significant association with residential segregation in Canada ($p<.1$).

---

an alpha of .05 provides a balance of the issue of statistical power with statistical errors.

Table 5.3 Regression results, Model I, U.S.

		$l(D)$	$l({_x}P{_x})$
Ethnic resources			
Acculturation		-.523 **	.294 **
Socioeconomic status		.241 **	-.329 **
Group size (logged)		-.040 **	.467 **
Self-employment		.540 *	-1.206 **
	Constant	-.345 **	-7.597 **
	Adjust R^2	.507 **	.650 **
	N	1,718	

*p<.1; ** p<.05

Table 5.4 Regression results, Model I, Canada

		$l(D)$	$l({_x}P{_x})$
Ethnic resources			
Acculturation		-.592 **	.010
Socioeconomic status		-.034	-.272 **
Group size (logged)		-.078 **	.538 **
Self-employment		-.802	-.715
	Constant	.291	-8.409 **
	Adjust R^2	.671 **	.665 **
	N	189	

*p<.1; ** p<.05

This first statistical model accounts for more than 50 per cent of the variation in both indices of ethnic residential segregation in each country. Much of the difference in ethnic residential patterns then, can be attributed to differences in resources between groups. But the effect of these resources, without controlling for the urban context, panethnic membership or geographic region, varies depending on the segregation dimension being discussed, evenness or exposure. That is, both acculturation and socioeconomic status were expected to have integrating effects on ethnic groups, but this is not observed in the data. Rather, they appear to be operating differently on residential segregation according to the measure.

The first model also provides evidence of some cross-national differences and similarities. For example, group size operates on each index in similar ways across the two host societies. However, the U.S. and Canada do not experience segregation in quite the same way when it comes to the effect of self-employment, acculturation and socioeconomic status without controlling for the urban context, panethnic membership and geographic region.

When covariates are introduced into the model (Model II, Tables 5.5 and 5.6), we observe more consistent effects in the ethnic resource coefficients across the two segregation indices for each country, with the exception of group size. Acculturation scores have the expected negative association with both indices in both countries, holding constant metropolitan context, panethnic membership and geographic region. In other words, ethnic groups that are highly acculturated are likely to have lower levels of residential segregation in the urban areas of Canada and the United States.

The national context appears to be more relevant for the socioeconomic status factor. Net of covariates, ethnic groups with greater socioeconomic resources appear to be more residential segregated in the metropolitan areas of the United States (Model II, Table 5.5). In contrast, a statistically significant negative association appears in Model II for Canada (Table 5.6). This goes against expectations that the assimilationist paradigm would have an integrating effect in the U.S. and that the pluralist paradigm in Canada would have a retentionist or concentrating effect on ethnic residential patterns. Self-employment also varies by national context, having a segregating effect in the U.S. but no statistically significant association in Canada.

Table 5.5 Regression results, Model II, U.S.

	$l(D)$	$l(_xP_x)$
Ethnic resources		
Acculturation	-.281 **	-.330 **
Socioeconomic status	.100 **	.073 **
Group size (logged)	-.264 **	.915 **
Self-employment	.685 **	.971 **
Panethnicity		
White (omitted)	--	--
Black	.874 **	.798 **
Asian	-.233 **	-.120 **
Metropolitan context		
Population size (logged)	.425 **	-.798 **
Home ownership	-.437 **	.121
New housing	-1.709 **	-1.502 **
Industry (3 or more omitted)	--	--
0	.009	.001
1	.076 **	.007
2	.068 **	.022
Region		
West (omitted)	--	--
Midwest	.033	.090 **
Northeast	.004	.040
South	.170 **	.075 **
Constant	-3.637 **	-1.171 **
Adjust R^2	.808 **	.925 **
N	1,718	

*p<.1; ** p<.05

Table 5.6 Regression results, Model II, Canada

	$l(D)$	$l(_xP_x)$
Ethnic resources		
Acculturation	-.288 **	-.229 **
Socioeconomic status	-.077 *	-.145 **
Group size (logged)	-.277 **	.855 **
Self-employment	-.548	-.478
Panethnicity		
White (omitted)	--	--
Black	.156	-.038
Asian	.340 **	.159 **
Metropolitan context		
Population size (logged)	:432 **	-.718 **
Home ownership	-.189	.122
New housing	-1.483	-1.373
Industry (3 or more omitted)	--	--
1	-.032	-.059
2	-.084	-.044
Region		
Ontario (omitted)	--	--
Québec	.292 *	.346 **
BC & Prairies	.000	-.015
Maritimes	-.219	.013
Constant	-3.651 **	-1.632 **
Adjust R^2	.843 **	.917 **
N	189	

*p<.1; ** p<.05

Turning to panethnic grouping, Model II shows some clear cross-national patterns. Using White ethnic groups as the reference category, the segregation levels of Black ethnic groups in Canada are not different. Asian subgroups, however, appear to have much higher levels than White subgroups. The reverse is true in the U.S. results, which show that Asian ethnic groups are less segregated than White ethnic groups. Black subgroups' segregation levels are significantly higher in the U.S. Such a clear panethnic patterning in the results demonstrates that the panethnic or racial structure of society is important to understanding where groups locate spatially in relation to one another.

Studies of residential processes have shown that resources may operate in different ways for different groups suggesting that panethnicity or race should have an interacting effect with resources on integration (Alba and Logan 1993; Fong and Gulia 1999; Massey and Denton 1987; White and Sassler 2000). Model III in Tables 5.7 and 5.8 includes an interaction term with the acculturation and socioeconomic factors and with some exceptions, the patterns observed in Model II remain in Model III, where greater than 81 per cent of the variation in ethnic residential segregation is explained by the explanatory variables. These variables provide a solid explanation of the variation in levels of metropolitan residential patterns.

For the U.S. (Table 5.7), acculturation scores vary by panethnic grouping and while they have a negative association with residential segregation for all groups, they appear to have a stronger negative association for Black and Asian ethnic groups than for White subgroups. That is, although the negative effect for White ethnic groups is statistically significant, it does not translate into a large gain in residential integration with members outside of the ethnic group as compared to Blacks and Asians. This is evident in the graphs depicting this relationship, net of covariates, in Figure 5.3.[10] Along the horizontal axis is the acculturation score (which does not have any inherent meaning other than that higher values indicate higher levels of acculturation) and the vertical axis measures the segregation index converted back from the logit transformation.[11]

---

[10] Values for covariates are as follows: metropolitan population 1,000,000 (logged), homeownership .65, new housing construction .10, 2 industries, West region in the U.S., Ontario in Canada, group size 10,000 (logged), self-employment .10, acculturation score 0, socioeconomic score 0.

[11] See Chapter Four.

Table 5.7 Regression results, Model III, U.S.

	$l(D)$	$l(_xP_x)$
Ethnic resources		
Acculturation	-.113 **	-.179 **
Socioeconomic status	.179 **	.099 **
Group size (logged)	-.278 **	.895 **
Self-employment	.137	.580 **
Panethnicity		
White (omitted)	--	--
Black	.842 **	.935 **
Asian	-.266 **	-.253 **
Metropolitan context		
Population size (logged)	.425 **	-.786 **
Home ownership	-.559 **	-.008
New housing	-1.717 **	-1.505 **
Industry (3 or more omitted)	--	--
0	.011	.001
1	.076 **	-.005
2	.066 **	-.020
Region		
West (omitted)	--	--
Midwest	.015	.066 **
Northeast	-.021	.012
South	.144 **	.051 **
Interactions		
Acculturation*Black	-.141	-.186 **
Acculturation*Asian	-.296 **	-.328 **
SES*Black	-.210 **	.079
SES*Asian	-.107 **	-.005
Constant	-3.461 **	-1.110 **
Adjust R^2	.817 **	.928 **
N	1,718	

*p<.1; ** p<.05

Table 5.8 Regression results, Model III, Canada

	$l(D)$	$l(_xP_x)$
Ethnic resources		
Acculturation	-.339 **	-.256 **
Socioeconomic status	-.024	-.087
Group size (logged)	-.263 **	.866 **
Self-employment	-.120	-.232
Panethnicity		
White (omitted)	--	--
Black	.271	.047
Asian	.486 **	.217 **
Metropolitan context		
Population size (logged)	.395 **	-.747 **
Home ownership	-.352	-.006
New housing	-1.430	-1.394
Industry (3 or more omitted)	--	--
1	-.060	-.081
2	-.091	-.049
Region		
Ontario (omitted)	--	--
Québec	.325 **	.370 **
BC & Prairies	-.039	-.042
Maritimes	-.213	.022
Interactions		
Acculturation*Black	.138	.245
Acculturation*Asian	.275 **	.150 **
SES*Black	.008	-.054
SES*Asian	-.165 *	-.140 *
Constant	-3.140 **	-1.229
Adjust R^2	.849 **	.919 **
N		189

*$p<.1$; ** $p<.05$

In contrast to the U.S. pattern, White ethnic groups in Canada appear to experience the greatest decline in residential segregation levels with greater acculturation compared with the other two panethnic groupings, although the coefficient for Black subgroups was not statistically significant for either index likely due to the small sample size (Model III, Table 5.8). This is illustrated in the steeper slope for White ethnic groups as compared to Black and Asian subgroups in Canada (Figure 5.3). In the U.S., the effect of acculturation for White ethnic groups is also negative but the magnitude of the coefficient is less than it is for comparable groups in Canada, and greater gains are made for Black and Asian ethnic groups in the U.S.

Model III in Tables 5.7 and 5.8 also shows that the effect of socioeconomic resources depends, to some extent, on the panethnic or racial grouping to which the ethnic group belongs. Figure 5.4 allows us to observe these associations more clearly with socioeconomic factor scores listed along the x-axis. As with acculturation, these values have no direct interpretation other than higher values suggest higher levels of socioeconomic resources such as income and education.

Results in the table for the U.S. show that, net of covariates, higher socioeconomic scores are associated with higher levels of residential segregation for White subgroups in the United States. For the Isolation Index, no statistical differences emerge in the effect of socioeconomic resources between White subgroups and the other two groupings. However, in terms of Dissimilarity, Model III reveals a flatter line for both Asian and Black ethnic groups as compared with White groups. The illustrations of these statistical results in Figure 5.4 reveal that Whites and Asians actually appear to face *increasing* levels of segregation with rising SES levels as shown in the upward slopes in both panels, net of other factors. For Black ethnic groups, the pattern is not consistent across the two segregation indices. Socioeconomic resources appear to have no net effect on unevenness but a positive net effect on isolation.

In Canada, the inclusion of an interaction term points to panethnic patterns as well. For White ethnic groups, socioeconomic resources appear to have no statistically significant effect on segregation, although it does fall in the negative direction (Model III, Table 5.8). Black ethnic groups appear to be similar to White subgroups but Asians follow a different pattern. The slopes in Figure 5.4 illustrate the stronger integrating effect of socioeconomic resources for Asian groups in Canada.

When acculturation and socioeconomic factor scores are zero, panethnic levels of segregation remain as in Model II. Overall, Asian groups are much more segregated than White groups in Canada but less segregated than Whites in the U.S. Blacks are more segregated than Whites in the U.S. context and in Canada, although for the latter the difference is not statistically significant.

In addition to panethnic differences in residential processes, we can also discern whether there are cross-national patterns from Figures 5.3 and 5.4 and evaluate them against the hypotheses specified in Chapter Three. I expected to find greater evidence of spatial assimilation for White ethnic groups in the U.S. compared to comparable groups in Canada. Looking at both of the lines for acculturation and socioeconomic status, the data do not support this first hypothesis. While acculturation does have the intended negative effect, socioeconomic status has a positive one. Moreover, acculturation has a greater effect on metropolitan residential segregation for these groups in Canada.

In order for the second hypothesis on Black ethnic groups to be supported, we should find at least socioeconomic status to be associated with persistent residential concentration for these groups in the U.S. The results do demonstrate persistent levels of segregation with respect to socioeconomic resources. However, it appears that with increasing acculturation, Black ethnic groups find themselves to be less residentially distinctive in metropolitan areas. For Black groups in Canada, there is evidence of ethnic retention, that is, persisting levels of residential concentration in spite of increasing acculturation and SES.

The hypothesis related to Asian ethnic groups is also partially supported. Like the other two U.S. panethnic groupings, there appears to be a tendency for spatial assimilation in the effect of acculturation for U.S. Asian groups but not in terms of socioeconomic status. In contrast, Asian groups in Canada reveal a pattern consistent with ethnic retention, as expected. Acculturation does not diminish ethnic residential distinctiveness for these groups in Canada. Rather, this is achieved through gains in socioeconomic status.

Figure 5.3 Acculturation

A. Net effect of acculturation scores on Dissimilarity

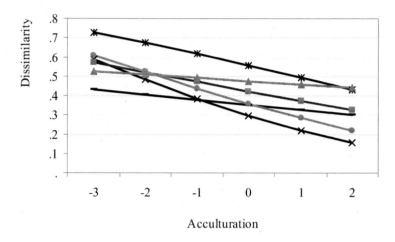

B. Net effect of acculturation scores on Isolation

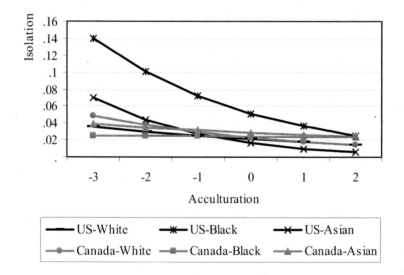

Figure 5.4 Socioeconomic resources

A. Net effect of socioeconomic scores on Dissimilarity

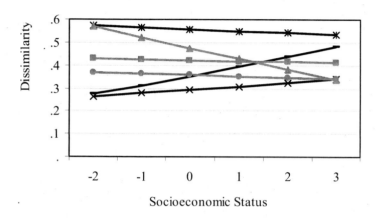

B. Net effect of socioeconomic scores on Isolation

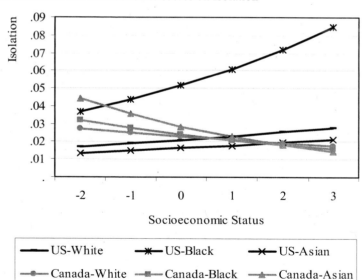

Comparing these three panethnic groupings across countries reveals the relevance of the national context. Residential incorporation processes are not consistent across comparable groupings in different countries. All three panethnic groups in the U.S. appear to follow a similar model of residential incorporation. That is, acculturation has a negative effect on levels of metropolitan residential segregation but not socioeconomic status. In Canada, groups are diverse in their residential incorporation patterns. Acculturation is negatively associated with concentration for White ethnic groups but not the others and socioeconomic resources are negatively associated with concentration for Asian ethnic groups but not the others.

In sum, three main findings emerge from these statistical tests. First, acculturation is a better predictor of residential intermingling than socioeconomic resources. For most groups in both countries, although to varying degrees, higher acculturation levels are associated with lower levels of residential segregation. On the other hand, higher SES scores – other than for Asians in Canada – are not associated with less segregation.

Second, with the appropriate control variables, the effect of the two key ethnic resource indicators, acculturation and socioeconomic status, are similar between Dissimilarity and Isolation. While the two indices tap into different dimensions of segregation, there appear to be some common residential processes across them. In other words, group factors associated with segregation – other than size – are generally consistent across indices. In the U.S., acculturation is associated with residential integration, and SES and self-employment are linked to segregation. In Canada, acculturation, SES and self-employment are all linked to integration.

Finally, there are cross-national differences in the way ethnic resources impact on ethnic residential segregation and these differences depend on panethnic boundaries. A systematic national pattern is found for U.S. groups. Groups that are more adapted culturally (i.e. language, nativity and age) are more likely to be less residentially conspicuous. However, they do not seem to "buy" integration with their socioeconomic resources. This is consistent across all three panethnic groupings in the U.S.

This section dealt specifically with the effect of ethnic resources on the two residential segregation measures. In the next part, I discuss the importance of the urban and regional context using the results from the same statistical tests before moving onto a closer examination of panethnic differences across countries.

The urban and regional context

The urban setting, through its history of social, economic and physical development, serves to structure residential outcomes, and this is borne out in the data. In both countries, population size operates on segregation patterns in the opposite direction as group size. Where larger group sizes are associated with lower levels of Dissimilarity and higher values of Isolation, the larger urban populations are associated with higher levels of Dissimilarity and lower levels of Isolation. And these effects are the same across both countries (Model III in Tables 5.7 and 5.8).

This is consistent with expectations as larger cities are likely to offer opportunities for socially differentiated groups to find and establish separate residential spaces (White, Fong and Cai 2003). Yet, when it comes to interaction or exposure, ethnic groups in larger cities are likely to comprise much smaller proportions thereby increasing their probability of interacting with those from other groups and decreasing the probability of interacting with those from the same ethnic group.

With metropolitan population size, group characteristics and panethnic grouping controlled, other metropolitan factors have comparable effects on segregation in both countries, with the exception of the industrial base. Homeownership and new housing both contribute to lower levels of ethnic segregation. A less diversified industrial base contributes to an increased level of ethnic residential unevenness in the U.S. but not in Canada. [12]

Finally, geographic location of the metropolitan area is also important. Ethnic groups located in the urban areas in the U.S. South and Midwest are more residentially segregated than in the U.S. West. Comparing the Canadian provinces with Ontario, groups situated in the western and eastern regions generally appear to exhibit slightly lower

---

[12] A quick glance at the table for Canada will show a lack of statistical significance for these metropolitan variables. This result, despite relatively large coefficients, can partly be attributed to the limited number and variation of metropolitan areas in Canada. In the data, 25 out of 27 metropolitan areas are represented and in the data, Toronto and Vancouver are the most heavily weighted.

levels of segregation while those in Québec exhibit a significantly higher level.

CANADA VERSUS THE UNITED STATES:
PANETHNIC LEVELS OF SEGREGATION

In this section, I consider whether differences in the levels of ethnic residential segregation by panethnicity and national context can be explained by differences in ethnic resources, metropolitan characteristics and geographic region. These results are based on a pooled model in Table 5.9 and shown graphically in Figure 5.5 for Dissimilarity and Figure 5.6 for Isolation, with the logits converted back to their original units. The top panels of both figures provide an aggregated summary by panethnicity the segregation statistics contained in Tables 5.1 and 5.2. The bottom panels reveal the level of segregation by panethnicity and country after controlling for covariates (refer to Note 10 in this chapter for constant values).

Figure 5.5, Panel B shows that once ethnic group factors, metropolitan context and geographic region are held constant, the cross-national gap in the level of Dissimilarity for White ethnic groups disappears. This is shown statistically in the unstandardized coefficient for Canada in Table 5.9. A further comparison of the two panels of Figure 5.5 shows that the lower initial level of Dissimilarity of Whites from the other groupings in both countries can be attributed to differences in the explanatory variables. Controlling for these factors, the unevenness level for Whites increased and decreased for the other two groups such that a comparable level is reached between Whites and Asians in both countries and between Whites and Blacks, and between Asians and Blacks in Canada (Figure 5.5, Panel B).

The gaps between countries for the other two groupings, Blacks and Asians, do not disappear after controlling for metropolitan and group traits (Figure 5.5, Panel B). The higher level of Dissimilarity for Blacks in the U.S. compared to their counterparts in Canada and the higher level of Dissimilarity for Asians in Canada compared to their counterparts in the U.S. suggests that segregation for these groups may be better explained by contextual factors in host societies and not differences in metropolitan areas or group characteristics.

Table 5.9 Regression results on residential integration, pooled sample

	$l(D)$	$l(_xP_x)$
Ethnic resources		
Acculturation	-.150 **	-.191 **
Socioeconomic status	.167 **	.090 **
Group size (logged)	-.280 **	.889 **
Self-employment	.094	.214
Panethnicity		
White (omitted)	--	--
Black	.789 **	.833 **
Asian	-.240 **	-.231 **
Metropolitan context		
Population size (logged)	.431 **	-.775 **
Home ownership	-.499 **	-.057
New housing	-1.082 **	-1.493 **
Industry (3 or more)	--	--
0	-.003	-.001
1	.062 **	.001
2	.044 *	.020
Interactions		
Acculturation*Black	-.097	-.154 *
Acculturation*Asian	-.240 **	-.274 **
SES*Black	-.230 **	.027
SES*Asian	-.119 **	-.018
Canada	.004	.031
Canada*Black	-.570 **	-.524 **
Canada*Asian	.524 **	.157 **
Constant	-3.525 **	-1.073 **
Adjust R^2	.813 **	.924 **
N		1,907

*p<.1; ** p<.05

Figure 5.5 Panethnic differences in Dissimilarity

A. Panethnic differences in Dissimilarity, without controls

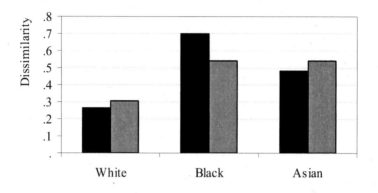

B. Net panethnic differences in Dissimilarity, pooled model

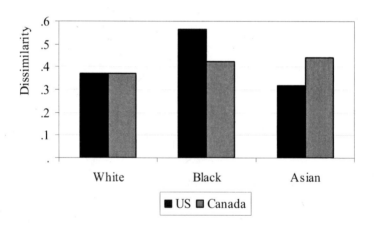

Figure 5.6 Panethnic differences in Isolation

A. Panethnic differences in Isolation, without controls

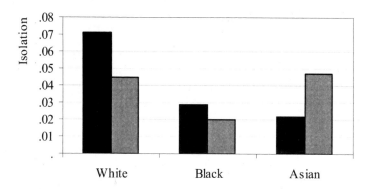

B. Net panethnic differences in Isolation, pooled model

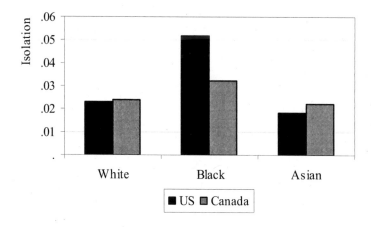

Figure 5.6, Panel B provides the same analysis, this time using the logit of the Isolation Index as the dependent variable (and converted back from the logit to the original scale in the graph). The cross-national gap in levels of isolation for White and Asian ethnic groups, respectively, are reduced with the inclusion of control variables but it becomes more pronounced for Black ethnic groups, with greater levels in the United States than Canada. In this graph, Whites and Asians present similar levels of Isolation and Black ethnic groups experience a much higher degree of exposure to their own group members than with others. This pattern is observed across the two societies.

The results from this analysis show that the national context is important for how panethnicity and race affect residential patterns, although not always in the direction predicted. We expected that the Canadian context would engender lower levels of segregation for ethnic groups in Canada than in the U.S. but this only applied for Black groups, and not for White or Asian ethnic groups.

SUMMARY AND DISCUSSION

This chapter opened with two questions regarding cross-national patterns of ethnic residential segregation and the effect of panethnicity or race. The data analysis shows that some groups are more segregated in one context than in another and that other groups experience similar levels across Canada and the United States. This pattern became clearer when ethnic groups were classified by panethnic membership. In general, Black ethnic groups are more segregated in the U.S. context than in Canada and Asian ethnic groups are more segregated in the Canadian context than in the U.S. Whites seem to share similar levels in both countries. These patterns emerge after controlling for ethnic group characteristics and the metropolitan context, and for both indices of segregation.

The findings also show that ethnic resources are important for predicting residential integration. This chapter identified four indicators, group size, self-employment rate, acculturation and socioeconomic resources, and highlighted the interacting effect of acculturation and socioeconomic resources with panethnic grouping in order to understand how the racial or panethnic structure of society shapes ethnic residential distinctiveness.

The statistical tests reveal that group level differences in acculturation and socioeconomic resources explain some of the variation in ethnic residential incorporation. But the effects of these variables depend on the panethnic grouping in which the ethnic group is subsumed. Acculturation emerges as a good predictor of residential dispersion or interaction for ethnic groups in both countries. However, there is no general process leading towards residential intermingling when socioeconomic resources are considered. This may be partly explained by the high levels of education and income brought over by immigrants who settle in ethnic residential neighborhoods as well as by a desire of some groups to maintain social separation and a sense of ethnic community through spatial separation. In the latter case, increased socioeconomic resources may "buy" separation. This is more evident in the U.S. than in Canada, where there is some weak evidence of residential dispersion, and evidence which is stronger for Asians than for other groups. For U.S. panethnic groupings, socioeconomic status appears to be a way for increasing separation, especially for Whites.

As expected, the three panethnic groups do not entirely share the same integration experience in the U.S., although they tend to share similar processes. This is the case for the groups in Canada as well with greater panethnic differences in the processes of incorporation. Integration processes did not always concur with expected directions. The national context did not have the expected effect on the association between ethnic resources and residential concentration for White ethnic groups, and only partial support for Asian and Black ethnic groups.

This pattern of residential integration suggests that the national context is important in more complex ways than first thought. It was argued that the national context supports dispersion in Canada more so than in the U.S., notwithstanding the melting pot and mosaic contrast. However, we find that this depends on panethnic grouping as well as the particular ethnic resource factor, acculturation or socioeconomic resources. This makes it difficult to disentangle the various aspects of the national context and its particular impact.

Nevertheless, the findings leave us with some initial thoughts regarding the relevance of the national context. First, the structure of inequality is important for explaining the differences in levels of residential segregation between Black ethnic groups in the U.S. and Canada. Second, ethnic retention is supported among Asian ethnic groups in Canada but not in the U.S., where pressures to assimilate have led to lower relative segregation levels. Levels for White ethnic groups do not appear to be sensitive to the national context as their levels were similar across national borders.

With respect to the process of residential incorporation, we find that the assimilationist orientation of U.S. society influences how acculturation changes residential distinctiveness especially for Black and Asian ethnic groups. These groups are more likely to follow the assimilation path than comparable groups in Canada, where they exhibit a greater tendency for retaining ethnic distinctiveness. Contrary to expectations, this feature of host societies does not appear to affect White ethnic group integration in the same manner.

With a host society context that supports residential concentration through family sponsorship obligations, informal settlement assistance and racial inequality, it is not surprising to find that improvements in socioeconomic status are not linked to declining levels of segregation for groups in the United States but rather, to increasing levels of segregation.

The settlement sector, characterized as an "industry" in Canada, offers newcomers information about housing, employment, healthcare, etc. By acting as a bridge between their ethnic community and the host society, the work of this sector may also have the effect of increasing interethnic interaction as immigrants improve their socioeconomic standing. This would operate through integration programs that inform newcomers about employment opportunities away from ethnic niches, programs that teach official languages and bring together immigrants from different places, and programs that inform newcomers about citizenship, civic participation and the multicultural nature of Canadian society. There is less of a settlement sector in the U.S., where newcomers often rely on local ethnic networks to help them adjust (Bloemraad 2003). For that reason, there are likely to be fewer opportunities to interact with non-group members. This also explains why the greater flows of family migrants in the U.S. context might contribute to increasing concentration.

The history and structure of racial inequality also helps our understanding of cross-national differences in the mechanisms that lead to residential distinctiveness that emerge in the analysis. With respect to Black ethnic groups, their levels of concentration remain despite increasing socioeconomic resources as expected. Although there is some degree of in-group preferences operating for middle-class Blacks, residential options for them still remains constrained (Adelman 2005; Pattillo 2005).

These results provide strong evidence that the relevance of the national context and group resources lies in regard to its panethnic structure. They argue for more nuanced questions regarding integration processes and whether assimilation, retention or stratification is the most valid theoretical paradigm for understanding ethnic relations. Questions regarding ethnic residential distinctiveness should now focus on several different factors including, What kind of ethnic resource is being considered, acculturation or socioeconomic resources? To which panethnic group does the ethnic group belong? And, where is the group located?

In addition to ethnic group characteristics and panethnicity, the metropolitan context and regional location are also important for understanding residential patterns in the metropolitan areas of Canada and the United States. Specifically, the population size of the metropolitan area is positively associated with an uneven ethnic group distribution and negatively associated with ethnic isolation. Ethnic groups located in metropolitan areas in the U.S. South and Québec in Canada are the most residentially segregated.

The foregoing analysis did not permit an analysis of the particular trajectories of individual ethnic groups in particular metropolitan areas. But, the results did demonstrate ethnic variation in residential distinctiveness within panethnic groupings as well as across metropolitan areas (and across countries). To get at a greater understanding of the ethnic dimension in residential integration, I focus on the experience of four specific ethnic groups in the neighborhoods of selected metropolitan areas in the following Chapters Six and Seven.

CHAPTER SIX

Narrowing the focus:
Four ethnic groups

Chapter Five provided a first glimpse of the group- and context-specific nature of residential integration. Ethnic groups revealed different experiences of residential integration in the metropolitan areas of two host societies according to their panethnic groupings, Asian, Black or White. The previous analysis also underscored the importance of group characteristics, the urban context and the national setting. These distinctions raise further questions about residential integration at a finer level of ethnic and geographic detail.

In this chapter and continued in Chapter Seven, I focus on the residential integration patterns of specific groups in selected metropolitan areas to examine whether pathways to integration are particular to ethnic groups and urban settings. To elucidate these ethnic residential processes, four ethnic groups are analyzed – the Chinese, Jamaicans, Iranians, and the Vietnamese – each in two metropolitan areas in two countries, Canada and the United States. Seven metropolitan areas are represented: Los Angeles, New York, San Francisco, Miami, Toronto, Montréal and Vancouver. The four contrasting groups have been selected for their relatively large population sizes, differential experiences of migration, host and sending country relations, racial grouping and cultural or religious orientation.

A short migration history of each group to Canada and the United States is described in the next section, explaining the rationale for their selection. Subsequent sections deal with data, sample, variables and methods. Chapter Seven discusses the results of the statistical analysis.

CHINESE

The two countries share similar experiences with immigration from China. The first large wave of migrants arrived first to the U.S. and then to Canada in the mid-1800s in response to the discovery of gold on the west coast (Con, Con, Johnson, Wickberg, and Willmott 1982; Lyman 1974; Tung 1974). Political and economic linkages between the countries facilitated these migrations. As part of the *Treaty of Nanking* in 1842, an agreement between Britain and China, subjects were provided access to each other's lands, which included Canada. The 1844 *Treaty of Wanghsia* between China and the United States preceded the first large wave to America. Subsequently, the Chinese were recruited to work in railroad construction in both countries. The second significant period of migration occurred in the mid-1900s after exclusionary policies were repealed, which took 60 years in the U.S., from 1882 to 1943, and 25 years in Canada, from 1923 to 1947 (Con et al. 1982; Lin 1998).

In contrast with the earliest migrants, who mostly came from rural areas in southern China, those in the recent period are likely to have arrived from urban areas such as Hong Kong (Li 1988). Another significant change is in the attitudes toward Chinese immigrants, which have become more favorable compared with the discriminatory policies and practices of the past, with both governments now actively recruiting Chinese migrants (Holland 2007). The Chinese form a significant Asian ethnic group in Canada and the U.S. with a long history of seeking better economic opportunities in metropolitan areas, and they cannot be overlooked in a study of ethnic integration.

JAMAICANS

Jamaicans have been migrating to North America since the early 1900s. Yet, large migration flows to North America only began in the 1960s, after Britain closed its borders by enacting a restrictive immigration policy in 1962, and the United States and Canada repealed their own restrictive policies (Thompson and Bauer 2003). Like others from the Caribbean, many left Jamaica as labor migrants, seeking economic opportunities and a sense of achievement. This is perpetuated by a culture of migration that is rooted in Jamaica's institutions (Maingot 1991; Thomas-Hope 2002).

Programs encouraging emigration from Jamaica are also similar across the two countries. Males have been recruited to work on farms –

in sugar fields and fruit harvesting in Florida and the mid-West, and on fruit, vegetable and tobacco farms in Canada – and females arrived to work in domestic service and as nurses. Many researchers note the skilled or semi-skilled nature of migration from Jamaica and the white-collar background of many of the immigrants (Foner 1985; Thomas-Hope 2002).

Jamaicans present an interesting immigrant group for this study due to their English-language ability, which should lead to high levels of integration in both the United States and Canada. But this language advantage is tempered by the racial marker of the majority of migrants and the racial structures that greet them. As one of the largest Black immigrant groups in either country, their adaptation experience will be informative.

IRANIANS

Migration to North America from Iran is generally grouped into two waves, demarcated by the Iranian revolution in 1979. Prior to the establishment of the Islamic regime in Iran, Iranians moved to Canada and the United States in hopes of achieving mostly educational objectives (Bozorgmehr and Sabagh 1988; Shahidian 1999). After the revolution, many Iranians were forced to leave Iran, seeking asylum in North America among other places. The reasons and motivations for emigration from Iran then, are varied, as are the political and religious beliefs the emigrants carry.

Iranians are comprised of at least 4 ethno-religious sub-groups, including Muslims, Jews, Armenians and Bahais, whose experience as a majority or minority group in Iran have had some implications for their level of ethnic retention in the United States. Bozorgmehr (1997) argues that minority groups in Iran such as Jews, Armenians and Bahais, have stronger co-ethnic ties in the U.S. than Muslims, the majority group in Iran. However, despite these sub-ethnic differences, or what Bozorgmehr (1997) refers to as "internal ethnicity," there is evidence to suggest that a somewhat cohesive Iranian community and identity has formed through "collective remembrance and nostalgia" (Mostofi 2003) as well as language (Hoffman 1989; Modarresi 2001).

For these reasons, Iranians are a fascinating case for the study of integration. Although a smaller group than Chinese or Jamaicans, comparing their residential integration patterns in Canada and the United

States against the backdrop of differential ethnic and racial classification schemes and host society receptions, will provide a unique opportunity for the examination of contextual and ethnic group influences. In the United States, Iranians are classified as a white ancestry group and in Canada, Iranians are not considered to be white, but a visible minority. Moreover, the anti-Iranian stance of the U.S. and state government, propagated by the U.S. media (Kelley 1991), which is, for the most part, lacking in the Canadian context, is likely to play some role in the integration patterns of Iranians.

VIETNAMESE

Relatively few Vietnamese were in North America prior to the refugee movement in the mid-to-late 1970s. The first period of sizable migration, to both Canada and the United States, took place between 1975 and 1977 when the U.S. withdrew its military support and the South Vietnamese government lost power to the Communist North (Do 1999; Dorais 1991). The second wave, mostly of the ethnic Chinese in Vietnam, began soon afterwards in 1978 in response to the harsh policies of the Communist government.

Vietnamese refugees from both periods were not welcomed with open arms in either host society but international attention and the political involvement of Canada and the U.S. in Vietnam impelled governmental intervention. In Canada, governmental assistance took the form of resettlement, material assistance, language training and employment counseling (Adelman 1982). Similar programs were offered in the United States, with state and voluntary organizations providing income support, medical care and other social services (Hein 1995). The particular reception of the Vietnamese, their reasons for migration, their short history in both places and their identity as an Asian ethnic group present an interesting contrast to the other groups, particularly the Chinese.

The four ethnic groups present a contrast in terms of racial traits, motives for migration, and host society reception. Given these distinctive experiences, ethnic groups cannot be expected to have identical residential outcomes.

The Chinese, migrating to North America primarily for economic reasons, may be expected to disperse residentially with increasing ethnic resources. Their long history of migration to the continent, political and economic linkages between China and each of the two countries, and the favorable climate for Chinese migration in recent times argue for an ethnic group with the motivation and opportunity to residentially assimilate in both contexts. Yet, this predilection may be hindered by their non-White status and the integration policies of Canada and the United States.

Jamaicans form another ethnic group whose motivation for migration is largely for labor purposes. This context of migration and the lack of a language barrier would argue for the residential integration of this group in both countries. Yet, their position as a Black ethnic group is likely to result in high levels of concentration in both places, although this may be more common in U.S. metropolitan areas due to the more prominent history of Black racial segregation and racial conflict.

Iranians in U.S. metropolitan areas, on the one hand, may be expected to conform to an assimilationist path of residential integration, as they are classified as a White ethnic group. On the other hand, two other forces likely to impinge on residential patterns suggest otherwise; the large composition of refugees and anti-Iranian sentiment. In Canada, the categorization of Iranians as a visible minority and their refugee flows may make them less likely to be residentially dispersed and more likely to remain concentrated with other co-ethnics.

The Vietnamese are also primarily refugees to both countries. Like the Iranians, this context of migration suggests that the Vietnamese may prefer to maintain strong ties with their ethnic group as they have been forced to leave their country of origin. However, the favorable reception in the form of governmental intervention and assistance may push the Vietnamese to integrate with those outside of the ethnic community. Given the patterns by panethnicity we observed in the previous analysis (Chapters Four and Five), it will be interesting to contrast this Asian ethnic group with the Chinese.

These four groups are highly concentrated in a handful of metropolitan areas in each country. This argues for a closer examination of these groups in those areas. In Tables 6.1 and 6.2, the top two metropolitan areas for each of the four ethnic groups are listed as are the levels of segregation as determined by the Dissimilarity Index. As described below, members of different ethnic groups are drawn to similar cities: Los Angeles, New York, San Francisco and Miami in the U.S.; and Toronto, Vancouver and Montréal in Canada.

New York and San Francisco house the largest ethnic communities for the Chinese (22 and 20 per cent, respectively, of all Chinese in the U.S.). In Canada, the largest communities of Chinese reside in Toronto (42 per cent of all Chinese in Canada) and Vancouver (34 per cent). This translates to about 490,000 Chinese in New York, 460,000 in San Francisco and about 380,000 in Toronto and 310,000 in Vancouver (Tables 6.1 and 6.2). Despite having the smallest community in Vancouver, the Chinese have a much larger presence there, comprising 16 per cent of the metropolitan population. Figure 6.1 graphs the Chinese in the four metropolitan areas along a number of selected social, economic and demographic traits, which shows that the Chinese communities are comparable, with relatively even proportions of females, legally married (of those 15 years and older) and older adults (65 years and over). However, relatively large differences are visible in the proportion foreign-born and in educational attainment, especially between Vancouver and New York, with the Vancouver Chinese having lower proportions of those over 25 years of age with university degrees. San Francisco, having the oldest Chinese settlement in North America, has the lowest proportion foreign-born of the four areas, although it is still over 65 per cent. Of those foreign-born, there appears to be a cross-national pattern in the timing of arrival, with the two Canadian metropolitan areas tending to have larger proportions of more recent immigrants. The Chinese in these areas are also more likely to be self-employed.

The similar profiles of the community in the four metropolitan areas suggest that there may not be any difference in the degree of residential integration for the Chinese if group characteristics are the determining factor. A metropolitan level measure of residential segregation, the Dissimilarity Index,[13] shows that while the level of segregation is moderate, the differences across the four areas is negligible, .6 in New York, .51 in San Francisco, .54 in Toronto and .51 in Vancouver. This suggests that in all four places, more than half of the Chinese population would have to be re-distributed across neighborhoods (i.e. tracts) to achieve an even distribution.

---

[13] The Dissimilarity Index was calculated for each group in each metropolitan area in Chapter Four.

Table 6.1 Four ethnic group populations in selected metros, U.S.

US	Metros	Population	Percent of Group	Percent of Metro	D
Chinese	New York	493,046	21.8	.02	.60
	San Francisco	459,671	20.3	.07	.51
Jamaicans	New York	307,499	45.4	.01	.66
	Miami	113,342	16.0	.03	.53
Iranians	Los Angeles	101,292	32.4	.006	.70
	San Francisco	33,595	10.2	.005	.57
Vietnamese	Los Angeles	233,573	21.3	.014	.60
	San Francisco	146,613	13.4	.02	.58

Table 6.2 Four ethnic group populations in selected metros, Canada

Canada	Metros	Population	Percent of Group	Percent of Metro	D
Chinese	Toronto	379,550	41.8	.08	.54
	Vancouver	312,185	34.4	.16	.51
Jamaicans	Toronto	150,840	79.3	.03	.44
	Montréal	10,120	4.9	.003	.75
Iranians	Toronto	41,293	48.7	.009	.59
	Vancouver	20,485	25.0	.01	.57
Vietnamese	Toronto	34,200	30.6	.007	.58
	Montréal	21,650	19.5	.006	.60

Figure 6.1 Selected characteristics of the Chinese in four metropolitan areas

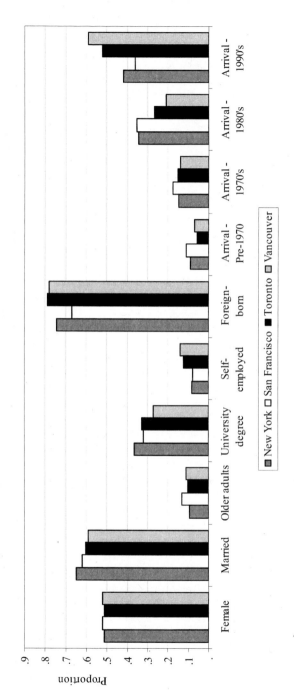

Figure 6.2 Selected characteristics of Jamaicans in four metropolitan areas

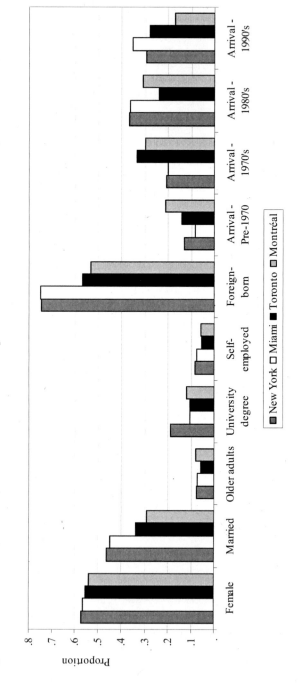

Most Jamaicans in the U.S. can be found in either New York (45 per cent) or Miami (16 per cent). Toronto is an overwhelmingly preferred choice for Jamaicans in Canada (79 per cent) and Montréal is a distant second (5 per cent). Jamaicans comprise equivalent proportions of Toronto's and Miami's population and they are the most numerous in New York at 310,000, at more than twice the size of the other two (Tables 6.1 and 6.2). Montréal has the second largest Jamaican community in Canada with over 10,000, but it is small in absolute terms, only one tenth the size of Toronto's own Jamaican community.

In terms of their characteristics, Jamaicans across the four metropolitan areas appear to be somewhat similar, with the sharpest contrasts occurring in the proportion married, proportion with a university degree, proportion foreign-born and timing of arrival for the foreign-born (Figure 6.2). With the exception of educational attainment, the differences largely vary by country. Jamaicans in the two Canadian metropolitan areas are less likely to be married, less likely to be foreign-born and more likely to have arrived earlier than those in New York or Miami. The most university educated Jamaican community is situated in New York.

As found in past studies (Jones 2008), these profiles demonstrate that Jamaican communities in various places are not all the same. This assertion holds for the degree of residential segregation as well. The Dissimilarity Indices in Tables 6.1 and 6.2 tell us that Jamaicans in New York and Montréal are more segregated at .66 and .75, respectively, than in Miami (.53) and Toronto (.44).

Los Angeles and San Francisco emerge as major areas of metropolitan concentration for Iranians (32 and 10 per cent, respectively). Just under half of the Iranian population in Canada is located in Toronto (49 per cent) followed by about one quarter in Vancouver (25 per cent). The largest concentration of Iranians in North America is found in the Los Angeles CMSA. Toronto is second with 42,000 Iranians and is followed by San Francisco and Vancouver. As suggested by the proportional values, Iranians are likely to have a slightly stronger presence in Canada. Figure 6.3 reveals that the four metropolitan areas have been attracting Iranian migrants differentially and there is evidence of some cross-national patterns. There is a greater proportion foreign-born in Toronto and Vancouver and the foreign-born are clearly more recent arrivals in Canada, with a large fraction arriving in the 1990s. Immigrant flows to Los Angeles and San Francisco were the greatest in the 1970s and 1980s. Los Angeles Iranians are also conspicuous for their higher proportion of members 25 years of age and over with a university degree and higher proportion self-employed.

There are modest differences in the four Iranian communities, as illustrated in Figure 6.3, being shaped by immigration and adaptation patterns. In terms of their metropolitan level of residential segregation (Tables 6.1 and 6.2), using the Dissimilarity Index, Iranians in Los Angeles are the most segregated in L.A. (.7) and very similarly distributed across tracts in San Francisco (.57), Toronto (.59) and Vancouver (.57).

Like Iranians, the two most popular residential choices for the Vietnamese in the U.S. are Los Angeles and San Francisco (21 and 13 per cent, respectively). In Canada, the largest communities of Vietnamese are situated, not surprisingly, in Toronto (31 per cent). Montréal is a second area of concentration (20 per cent). As shown in Tables 6.1 and 6.2, the Vietnamese populations in the two U.S. metropolitan areas, 235,000 in L.A. and 147,000 in San Francisco, are much larger than in Toronto (35,000) and Montréal (22,000). Their presence is likely to be stronger in the U.S. as well as they comprise larger proportions in Los Angeles and San Francisco than in the two Canadian metros. In these U.S. metropolitan areas, the foreign-born Vietnamese are also more likely to be older arrivals than their counterparts in Toronto or Montréal (Figure 6.4). While generally similar in social and economic characteristics across all four metropolitan areas, those in Montréal are the most highly educated and are an older immigrant stream, with the majority of their foreign-born arriving in the 1970s and 1980s. The two U.S. metropolitan communities are also roughly similar to one another although the Vietnamese in Los Angeles have slightly higher levels of educational attainment.

Despite these slight differences in educational attainment and timing of migration, the Dissimilarity levels in the four areas are much the same, .6 in Los Angeles and Montréal and .58 in San Francisco and Toronto.

Figure 6.3 Selected characteristics of Iranians in four metropolitan areas

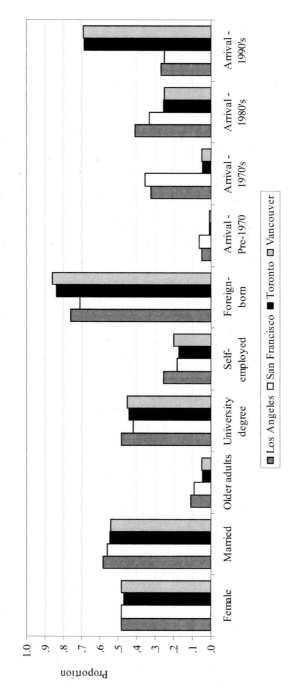

Figure 6.4 Selected characteristics of the Vietnamese in four metropolitan areas

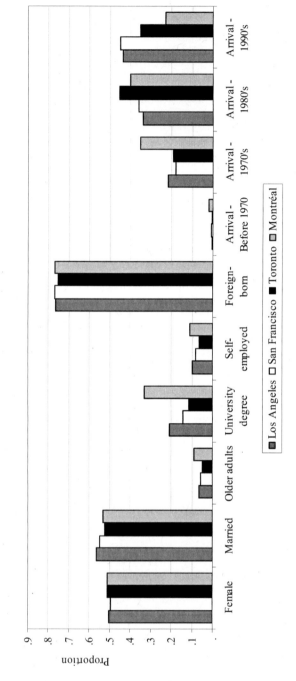

The unit of observation for each of the four ethnic groups in their relevant metropolitan areas is the census tract. The number of tracts used to analyze residential patterns at the neighborhood level varies for each ethnic group as it depends upon the distribution of each group within each metropolitan area represented. Tracts lacking at least one group member cannot be included. Moreover, the practice of data suppression does not permit the inclusion of tracts containing very small numbers of group members.[14]

For the Chinese, the minimum numbers in a tract are 196 for the New York CMSA and 126 for the San Francisco CMSA (Table 6.3). The minimum numbers of Jamaicans in a tract for the New York CMSA and Miami CMSA are 318 and 311, respectively (Table 6.3). For Iranian tracts (Table 6.4), the minimum numbers are 290 in the Los Angeles CMSA and 372 in San Francisco. Finally, the minimum numbers of Vietnamese are 271 and 300 for L.A. and San Francisco, respectively (Table 6.4). To maintain comparability, only tracts with at least 200 group members are included from the relevant Canadian census metropolitan areas.

The number of census tracts that are included in the multivariate analysis for each ethnic group is limited to those tracts that contain social and economic variables for that ethnic group in the U.S. census. The omission of all suppressed tracts resulted in a varying number of tracts for each metropolitan area and each ethnic group. For the U.S., the samples range from 42 tracts of Iranians in Los Angeles to 346 tracts of the Chinese in San Francisco. San Francisco is omitted from the analysis on Iranians due to the lack of tract level data (available for only 2 tracts). For the Chinese in Toronto 394 tracts are usable and at minimum 27 tracts in Vancouver for Iranians. Using the threshold of 200 for Canadian metropolitan tracts resulted in the omission of Montréal in the statistical analysis for Jamaicans and Vietnamese. Tables 6.3 and 6.4 list the sample sizes for each ethnic group.

The suppression of census tracts with lower numbers (and in

---

[14] The U.S. census bureau suppresses data in SF4 for ancestry/race groups in geographic areas with less than 50 unweighted cases. For some proportion of census tracts then, data on ethnic group characteristics are unavailable. This varies by ethnic group. In the case of Canada, most of these data are made available in the Statistics Canada custom tabulations.

general, lower proportions) of ethnic group members may create selectivity bias in the data. The exclusion of these tracts may bias the relationship since those tracts with the smallest proportions of group members (i.e. the most "integrated" group members) may also be linked in particular ways to ethnic traits. Although the majority of tracts contain at least one ethnic group member, the tracts included in the analysis generally capture a large proportion of group members as shown in the third row of each panel in Tables 6.3 and 6.4. The smallest proportions are .41 for Jamaicans in New York, .28 for Iranians in Los Angeles and .36 for the Vietnamese in Toronto. The results, albeit limited to a fraction of the ethnic group population and tracts, will still enable us to identify the association between resources and ethnic neighborhoods. To test for bias, I repeat the analysis for the ethnic groups in Canada using the more complete Canadian data in Appendix C.

DATA, SAMPLE SELECTION AND VARIABLES

I continue using the respective national censuses of Canada and the United States as described in Chapter Four. For this part of the analysis, census tract data were also extracted from the 2000 U.S. and 2001 Canadian censuses. From the U.S. census, relevant tables were obtained from Summary Files 3 and 4 for the relevant consolidated metropolitan statistical areas, and data on Canadian census metropolitan areas were purchased from Statistics Canada or downloaded from their website. The compiled dataset contains tract level data pertaining to individuals, and on the social and economic characteristics of the members of the four selected groups.

Ethnic groups in the study are defined by ethnic origin or ancestry as self-reported in the respective censuses of each country.[15] For ancestry groups in the U.S., SF4 tabulations are based on total ancestry counts.

---

[15] Although some internal differences within a given ethnic or ancestry group may be possible to identify for groups in Canada such as racial identification, place of birth, migration period or religion, comparable data are not available in the U.S. and there is a lack of research on the key dimensions of internal divisions for all of the ethnic groups. Despite internal diversity, these classifications, based on self-reports, are still useful for making comparisons and for maintaining consistency with past studies.

This applies to Iranians and Jamaicans, for whom all individuals of single and multiple ancestries are counted. The Chinese and Vietnamese counts in the U.S. are based on single ancestry as tabulations distinguish those who are of Asian origin alone or in combination. Comparable data for each of the groups are obtained from the census in Canada, which has a separate tabulation for single, multiple and total ancestry. For Iranians and Jamaicans, total response values are used and for the Chinese and Vietnamese, single origin tabulations are analyzed.[16]

The selective nature of immigration to specific urban areas argues for a study of particular groups in particular places. The two metropolitan areas in each country with the largest ethnic communities of each of the four groups are selected (Tables 6.1 and 6.2). Due to overlap, a total of seven metropolitan areas across both countries emerge as important destinations.

Dependent variable

The outcome of interest is the degree of ethnic residential distinctiveness at the neighborhood level. Once again integration is conceptualized as any community other than the co-ethnic community since we are interested in the degree to which ethnic groups maintain ethnic spaces. By residential distinctiveness, I refer to the degree to which ethnic group members live with co-ethnics in their neighborhoods. Empirically, this is measured as the proportion of one's own ethnic group in the census tract (Table 6.3). In the regression analyses, the logit of the proportions are taken due to their bounded nature and to normalize the distribution.[17]

---

[16] In Chapters Four and Five, single origin counts were used for all ethnic groups in Canada and first ancestry counts were used for particular groups in the U.S. Appendix B addresses the issue of data comparability. In this part of the analysis, single origin counts are preferable as they reflect actual numbers of people and not responses. However, to make the groups more comparable for this analysis, total response counts are used where relevant.

[17] See Chapter Four for the formula and for its conversion back to the original units.

Table 6.3 Sample sizes for Chinese and Jamaican samples

Chinese	New York	San Francisco	Toronto	Vancouver
Tracts in analysis	293	346	394	243
Minimum number in tracts	196	126	200	200
Proportion represented	0.53	0.73	0.89	0.96
Tracts with ethnic group	4,665	1,452	882	380
Total tracts in metro	5,072	1,455	924	386

Jamaicans	New York	Miami	Toronto	Montréal
Tracts in analysis	185	72	262	5
Minimum number in tracts	318	311	200	200
Proportion represented	0.41	0.57	0.7	0.12
Tracts with ethnic group	2,915	518	863	276
Total tracts in metro	5,072	623	924	846

Table 6.4 Sample sizes for Iranian and Vietnamese samples

Iranians	Los Angeles	San Francisco	Toronto	Vancouver
Tracts in analysis	42	2	47	27
Minimum number in tracts	290	372	200	200
Proportion represented	0.28	0.02	0.41	0.51
Tracts with ethnic group	1,389	776	603	241
Total tracts in metro	3,356	1,455	924	386

Vietnamese	Los Angeles	San Francisco	Toronto	Montréal
Tracts in analysis	133	97	36	15
Minimum number in tracts	271	300	200	200
Proportion represented	0.52	0.53	0.36	0.21
Tracts with ethnic group	2,903	1,385	492	420
Total tracts in metro	3,356	1,455	924	846

Tables 6.6 to 6.7 provide the descriptive statistics for each ethnic group by metropolitan area. The mean co-ethnic proportion (the dependent variable, prior to the logit transformation) of included tracts is indicated in the third row of each table. As these samples are restricted to those tracts for which we have data, these values are likely to be inflated. The average tracts in New York and San Francisco have similar proportions of Chinese at .19 (Table 6.6). In Toronto, the average tract included in the analysis contains about .16 proportion Chinese. It is greater in Vancouver, where there is .23 proportion Chinese.

For the other three groups, the mean tract proportion tends to be lower in Canadian metropolitan areas than in areas in the U.S. as well as generally being lower than for the Chinese. The mean group proportion of Jamaicans is the lowest in Toronto (.07) out of the three metropolitan areas represented (Table 6.6). The two Canadian metros have the lowest tract average for Iranians at .06 (Table 6.7) and the two U.S. metros have the highest levels for the Vietnamese at .16 in Los Angeles and .15 in San Francisco (Table 6.7).

Explanatory variables

Ethnic resources

The multidimensional nature of this key explanatory concept in this study is discussed in Chapter Four and is not repeated here. The same indicators at the metropolitan level used to run a principal components analysis are available for this level of investigation but when applied at the tract level for the seven metropolitan areas, no clear factor structure emerges. Instead, I operationalize this concept for this level of analysis using a single indicator for each of the two dimensions identified previously. For acculturation I use the proportion foreign-born and for socioeconomic status I use education, which is measured as the proportion of ethnic members 25 years of age and older with a university degree.[18] To maintain some consistency with the analysis in earlier

---

[18] The analysis was re-run using median male income and the results showed that the effect of income is similar to the effect of education for all of the ethnic groups except for Iranians in Vancouver, which revealed

chapters, I add the self-employment rate. The inclusion of these variables is supported by Figures 6.1 to 6.4, which show differences across ethnic groups and metropolitan areas along these dimensions. Variables and their measurements are listed in Table 6.5.

The descriptive statistics for the explanatory variables are presented for each ethnic group separately (Tables 6.6 and 6.7). The proportion foreign-born for each of the groups shows that the mean proportion foreign-born in tracts is similar across metropolitan areas with some cross-national differences. The Chinese in Toronto and Vancouver are more likely to be living in neighborhoods with a higher proportion of foreign-born Chinese than in New York or San Francisco. Jamaicans in Toronto are likely to be living in neighborhoods with a smaller proportion of foreign-born Jamaicans than Jamaicans living in New York or Miami. Iranians follow the same pattern as the Chinese, with a higher mean proportion of foreign-born co-ethnics in Toronto and Vancouver compared to Los Angeles. Finally, the Vietnamese are more likely to find themselves among foreign-born compatriots in Los Angeles and San Francisco than in Toronto. In most places, each of these ethnic groups are living in neighborhoods where greater than three quarters of their co-ethnic neighbors are immigrants.

The proportion with university degrees is also presented in Tables 6.6 and 6.7. Here we find greater variation across ethnic groups. The Chinese, in all four places, are likely to have about one-third of co-ethnics with university degrees. Jamaicans and Vietnamese share similar levels of university educated co-ethnic neighbors in their two U.S. metropolitan areas at about one in six and at about one in eleven in Toronto. Iranians are the most educated, with just less than half of co-ethnic neighbors with at least a Bachelor's degree or equivalent.

The self-employment rate is also the highest for Iranians, especially in Los Angeles where, on average, an Iranian is living in a neighborhood where 30 per cent of their Iranian neighbors are self-employed. In contrast, not one of the other groups find themselves residing among greater than 9 per cent of self-employed co-ethnic neighbors.

---

a positive association between median male income and residential concentration.

Table 6.5 Measurement of variables

Variables	U.S.	Canada
Residential concentration	Logit transformation of proportion co-ethnic in census tract	Logit transformation of proportion co-ethnic in census tract
Ethnic resources		
Foreign-born	Proportion foreign-born	Proportion immigrant and nonpermanent residents
Education	Proportion with university degree Bachelor's and above, 25+ yrs	Proportion with university degree Bachelor's and above, 25+ yrs
Self-employment	Proportion self-employed, 16+ yrs in labour force	Proportion self-employed, 15+ yrs in labour force
Neighborhood context		
Population size	Natural log of tract population	Natural log of tract population

Table 6.6 Descriptive statistics for the Chinese and Jamaican samples

Chinese	New York	San Francisco	Toronto	Vancouver
Number of tracts	293	346	394	243
Mean tract size, logged (std dev)	8.40 (-0.5)	8.54 (-0.4)	8.56 (-0.4)	8.56 (-0.3)
Mean group proportion (std dev)	.19 (-0.1)	.19 (-0.1)	.16 (-0.1)	.23 (-0.2)
Proportion foreign-born (std dev)	.76 (-0.08)	.68 (-0.1)	.77 (-0.08)	.77 (-0.08)
Proportion university degree (std dev)	.32 (-0.2)	.48 (-0.2)	.34 (-0.2)	.30 (-0.1)
Proportion self-employed (std dev)	.08 (-0.06)	.08 (-0.06)	.08 (-0.05)	.09 (-0.05)

Jamaicans	New York	Miami	Toronto	
Number of tracts	185	72	262	
Mean tract size, logged (std dev)	8.34 (-0.5)	8.85 (-0.4)	8.67 (-0.3)	
Mean group proportion (std dev)	.16 (-0.07)	.13 (-0.07)	.07 (-0.04)	
Proportion foreign-born (std dev)	.75 (-0.08)	.77 (-0.07)	.57 (-0.1)	
Proportion university degree (std dev)	.16 (-0.09)	.14 (-0.1)	.09 (-0.09)	
Proportion self-employed (std dev)	.05 (-0.04)	.08 (-0.05)	.04 (-0.04)	

Table 6.7 Descriptive statistics for the Iranian and Vietnamese samples

Iranians	Los Angeles	Toronto	Vancouver
Number of tracts	42	47	27
Mean tract size, logged (std dev)	8.59 (-0.3)	8.67 (-0.3)	8.81 (-0.2)
Mean group proportion (std dev)	.12 (-0.05)	.06 (-0.03)	.06 (-0.04)
Proportion foreign-born (std dev)	.80 (-0.1)	.88 (-0.07)	.89 (-0.07)
Proportion university degree (std dev)	.45 (-0.1)	.45 (-0.1)	.49 (-0.2)
Proportion self-employed (std dev)	.30 (-0.1)	.12 (-0.08)	.14 (-0.06)

Vietnamese	Los Angeles	San Francisco	Toronto
Number of tracts	133	97	36
Mean tract size, logged (std dev)	8.63 (-0.3)	8.62 (-0.3)	8.67 (-0.3)
Mean group proportion (std dev)	.16 (-0.1)	.15 (-0.08)	.06 (-0.03)
Proportion foreign-born (std dev)	.78 (-0.06)	.77 (-0.1)	.73 (-0.08)
Proportion university degree (std dev)	.17 (-0.1)	.19 (-0.1)	.07 (-0.06)
Proportion self-employed (std dev)	.08 (-0.06)	.07 (-0.05)	.02 (-0.04)

Neighborhood context

The neighborhood context such as its composition and history of settlement is also likely to be relevant for the settlement patterns of ethnic group members. While data on the composition of tracts are available, the small number of cases limits the variables that can be included. I use the tract population to control for the neighborhood context and the natural log of this variable is used in the analysis. The mean tract size ranges from about 4,000 to 7,000.

These patterns largely mimic earlier descriptive statistics (Figures 6.1 to 6.4) indicating that the sample reflects, to some extent, the larger community (although this is less the case for education).

Analytical Methods

Multivariate regression is applied to an ecological model of ethnic residential distinctiveness (logit of proportion co-ethnic in a tract) on ethnic resources and metropolitan area for each group separately, controlling for tract size. This design allows us to investigate the influence of ethnic characteristics on residential integration by metropolitan (and national) area. The unit of analysis in the model is the census tract and the model is given by the interaction equation:

$$\hat{C}_t = a + \sum_{i=1}^{3} b_i X_i + \sum_{j=1}^{3} d_j X_j + \sum_{i=1}^{3}\sum_{j=1}^{3} g_{ij} X_i X_j + h_k X_k$$

where $\hat{C}_t$ is the predicted value of the logit proportion co-ethnic in census tract t;

X_i is a series of ethnic resource variables, including proportion with a university degree, proportion foreign-born and proportion self-employed, all measured for ethnic group members in census tract t;

X_j is the metropolitan area as a series of dummy variables (a maximum of three additional areas plus the omitted); and

X_k is the logged population size of census tract t.

In the results, close attention is paid to the effects of the three ethnic resource indicators; proportion with a university degree, proportion foreign-born and proportion self-employed. This design allows us to investigate, to some extent, the influence of ethnic culture on residential integration. By controlling the ethnic group across different contexts, and their resources, similarities in residential outcomes may suggest that spatial proximity is valued by ethnic group members. Differences in outcomes, however, would provide support for the contention that the context is more important for how groups relate to themselves and to others.

Although at a lower scale of analysis than in the analysis described in the previous two chapters, the ecological implications of this model remain. As discussed in Chapter Four, the ecological model permits the examination of aggregate processes but limits inferences about individual behavior (Robinson 1950). For instance, one cannot apply a positive correlation between proportion Vietnamese and proportion of tract population with a university degree in census tracts to Vietnamese individuals. The modified ecological model used in this study (modified as it tests the proportion Vietnamese and proportion *Vietnamese* with a university degree in census tracts, along with other variables) also cannot be used to infer individual behavior. The findings will tell us to what degree educated ethnic group members cluster in ethnic neighborhoods. Finally, we must also be cautious in the interpretation of the regression results as the cross-sectional data only permit the examination of statistical associations, not causal ones.

CHAPTER SEVEN

Ethnic pathways to neighborhood integration

The extent to which ethnic residential integration follows the path predicted by the assimilation, stratification or retention model, or some combination, depends upon both ethnic factors and the social context, including the urban context as evident in the analysis in Chapter Five. This chapter examines the process of ethnic residential integration in neighborhoods with a focus on four specific ethnic groups, Chinese, Jamaicans, Iranians and Vietnamese, in selected metropolitan areas. I examine whether there are systematic differences in the factors that lead to residential distinctiveness for each of the four groups, which have been selected for their contrasting experiences of migration and host society reception, bilateral relations with the respective host society, panethnic or racial grouping and cultural or religious orientation.

The first section of this chapter provides a brief review of integration pathways as described in Chapter Two. Following that, in the second part of this chapter I present the results of the empirical analysis for each group. Each set of results shows to what extent acculturation and socioeconomic factors contribute to ethnic residential integration and compares patterns across metropolitan contexts in two countries, Canada and the United States. The last section is dedicated to a discussion of the results and their implications.

INTEGRATION PATHWAYS

The expected path to residential integration, for most ethnic groups, has been spatial assimilation. This perspective argues that ethnic groups are residentially distinctive because of cultural differences with other groups and the lack of socioeconomic resources that restrict residential mobility. Immigrant groups are expected to start off in ethnic neighborhoods and as they acculturate and improve their social and economic standing over time, residential dispersion should occur. This perspective predicts a negative association between ethnic resources and residential concentration.

Two competing perspectives explain why some groups may not adhere to the path expected by residential assimilation theory. One alternative explanation is identified by place stratification theory, which purports that the dual housing market restricts the residential choices of certain segments of society. Ethnic integration does not take place in a vacuum but, in the context of the United States, in a racially stratified social structure. Discrimination at all levels in the housing market direct racial groups into particular neighborhoods. According to this perspective, spatial assimilation operates for members of the dominant racial group. For others, steering by real estate agents, as a form of discrimination, leads to differential options and opportunities for housing (Galster 1990; Galster and Godfrey 2005). This accounts for continued residential concentration in spite of socioeconomic and acculturation gains. This approach predicts no change in the level of residential concentration by level of ethnic resources, and studies have mostly focused on the effect of socioeconomic status.

The first two perspectives share a fundamental premise that given the opportunity, people will convert resources into ethnically integrated neighborhoods. However, ethnic preferences can operate to draw co-ethnic group members together and with increasing resources may actually enhance ethnic group separation. This is the second alternative perspective and a third pathway of residential integration. The ethnic retention approach recognizes that through deliberate action, group members may actually choose to live in ethnic neighborhoods and predicts that ethnic resources could continue to facilitate or increase ethnic residential concentration.

In empirical testing, the spatial assimilation perspective highlights two factors, socioeconomic status and acculturation, to describe the process of residential integration. Clear evidence of this process, according to this perspective, would be supported by a negative association between each of these two factors and residential segregation. For ethnic retention to be a plausible explanation, the acculturation dimension should not be associated with decreasing segregation rates as this perspective argues that there is something about their shared experience and ethnic understanding that leads to the maintenance of residential spaces. Accordingly, for place stratification to be operating we should observe no association between socioeconomic status and residential distinctiveness. However, it must be stated that the presence of these associations does not prove the existence of either of the latter two processes but some interpretations can be offered.

The overall objective of this study is to explore whether ethnic residential integration is constant across different contexts and this second part of the analysis investigates this question with respect to particular ethnic groups in particular places. The results in previous chapters show that although group integration does not consistently fall in the direction expected, there are cross-national differences. There is a possibility that some of these unexpected findings might be related to aggregate effects (we pooled ethnic groups into three panethnic groupings, Black, White or Asian) and a closer examination is warranted. Chapter Two exposited some hypotheses that were tested in Chapter Five, and I test them again using a more narrow definition of ethnicity, that of national origins.

FOUR ETHNIC EXPERIENCES

Chinese

Table 7.1 presents the results of four statistical models using the Chinese sample of census tracts pooled across the four metropolitan areas. Model I shows the effect of educational attainment by metropolitan area on the logit of proportion co-ethnic, our indicator of residential concentration at this level of analysis. This first model shows that, in New York, as the proportion of Chinese with university degrees in a neighborhood increases, the lower the proportion of Chinese in the neighborhood. This effect is similar across Los Angeles, San Francisco and Vancouver but significantly different in Toronto. Not only are Toronto's Chinese significantly less concentrated, educational attainment also does not have as much of an integrating effect as it does in the other three areas.

Model II in the same table reveals the effect of proportion foreign-born on residential concentration with the metropolitan interaction. As expected, the proportion of foreign-born Chinese in a neighborhood is positively associated with concentration in New York and in Toronto and Vancouver but the effect is significantly less positive for those in San Francisco.

The effect of self-employment is isolated in Model III and although a negative coefficient is observed for New York, it is not statistically significant. However, there are significant metropolitan differences in the effect of self-employment. In San Francisco and Toronto, the proportion of self-employed Chinese in a neighborhood is positively associated with the co-ethnic proportion. In contrast, the effect of Vancouver's self-employment rate is negative.

When tract population and the three ethnic resource variables are included in Model IV, no significant metropolitan differences in the effect of education remain although the Toronto Chinese remain much less concentrated initially. Figure 7.1 illustrates the net effects of education by metropolitan area with the logit converted back to proportions.[19] Despite the initial differences between metropolitan areas, the first graph shows the generally integrating effect of education for the Chinese, controlling for the proportion of foreign-born Chinese, proportion of self-employed Chinese and census tract population.

The full model did not eliminate all differences in the effect of proportion foreign-born by metropolitan area. While still positive for the Chinese in all four places, those in Toronto and Vancouver make much greater gains in concentration than those in New York, although the coefficient for Vancouver is not significantly different from the latter. This can be observed visually. All four lines in Figure 7.2 are positive and although Toronto is statistically different from New York, the magnitude of the effect on proportion co-ethnic does not provide substantial evidence that there are real differences in the two cities. All four lines follow the path predicted by the spatial assimilation model.

As in Model III, the effect of self-employment is highly varied across metropolitan areas having no significant association in the two U.S. metros and opposite effects in each of the Canadian metros, net of covariates (Figure 7.3). This full model explains 23 per cent of the variation, an improvement over the other three reduced models.

---

[19] Results for all net effects control for proportion university degree (.3), proportion foreign-born (.3), proportion self-employed (.1) and census tract size (5,000). See Chapter Four for the conversion formula from a logit value back to a proportion.

Table 7.1 Regression of logit proportion Chinese on group characteristics and metropolitan area

Chinese	Model 1	Model 2	Model 3	Model 4
Metropolitan area (NY omitted)				
San Francisco	–	–	–	.697
	.063	1.192 **	-.179	
Toronto	-.636 **	-1.126 *	-.489 **	-2.425 **
Vancouver	.270	.428	.640 **	-.026
Proportion univ. degree	-1.599 **	–	–	-1.087 **
Degree*San Francisco	.386	–	–	.074
Degree*Toronto	.992 **	–	–	-.050
Degree*Vancouver	-.529	–	–	-.548
Proportion foreign	–	3.010 **	–	1.664 **
Foreign*San Francisco	–	-1.405 *	–	-.700
Foreign*Toronto	–	.966	–	2.589 **
Foreign*Vancouver	–	-.420	–	.995

cont'd next page

Table 7.1 (cont'd) Regression of logit proportion Chinese on group characteristics and metropolitan area

cont'd from previous page

Chinese	Model 1	Model 2	Model 3	Model 4
Proportion self-employed	-	-	-.944	-.212
Self*San Francisco	-	-	2.161 *	1.478
Self*Toronto	-	-	2.011	2.424 **
Self*Vancouver	-	-	-5.184 **	-4.137 **
Tract size (logged)	-	-	-	-.535 **
Constant	-1.137 **	-3.932 **	-1.575 **	1.949 **
Adjust R^2	.110 **	.100 **	.050	.230 **
N		1,276		

*p<.1; ** p<.05

Figure 7.1 Net effect of proportion university degree on proportion Chinese in census tracts

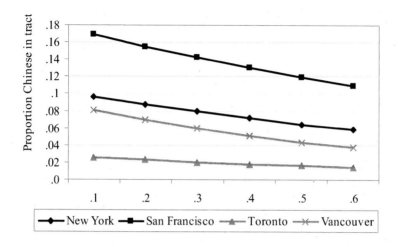

Figure 7.2 Net effect of proportion foreign-born on proportion Chinese in census tracts

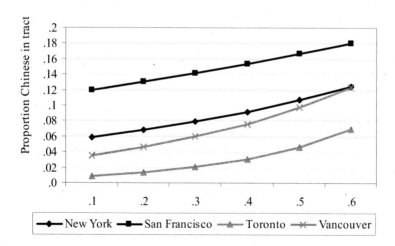

Figure 7.3 Net effect of proportion self-employed on proportion Chinese in census tracts

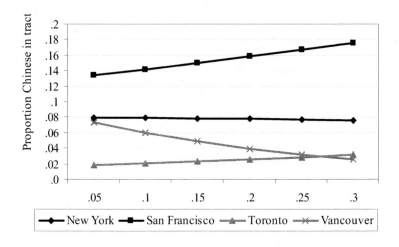

These results provide evidence of an assimilation path taken by the Chinese, which is consistent across metropolitan areas although the degree to which this is followed varies by the urban context. Nevertheless, the indicators for acculturation and socioeconomic status both show a general tendency for residential dispersion despite differences in the urban and national context. This is an indication that for the Chinese, residential distinctiveness is likely to diminish with increasing ethnic resources.

Jamaicans

Four statistical models using the Jamaican samples pooled across three metropolitan areas are presented in Table 7.2. Due to the lack of census tracts with adequate data, Montréal was removed from this part of the analysis. Results from the interaction models on the logit of proportion Jamaican show that the effect of education varies by metropolitan area (Model I). Socioeconomic resources, in terms of educational attainment, are not associated with residential concentration for Jamaicans in New York but are associated for Jamaicans in Miami and Toronto in a negative direction. The significant negative coefficient for Toronto suggests that Jamaican neighborhoods initially house a lower proportion there than in the two U.S. metros.

The effect of proportion foreign-born Jamaican in Model II shows a positive association with residential concentration for New York and a similar effect for Miami. This is different for Jamaicans in Toronto where neighborhoods with a small proportion of foreign-born Jamaicans have a similar co-ethnic proportion as neighborhoods with a large proportion of foreign-born Jamaicans. Model III presents the results for self-employment and it shows no statistically significant association between self-employment and residential patterns and also shows that the metropolitan area is less important.

The proportion of university educated Jamaicans does not appear to be a significant predictor of residential integration in New York or Miami, controlling for the other variables, although the slope for Miami is negative in Figure 7.4. (The small sample size (n=72 tracts) may explain the lack of statistical significance for Miami.) Education does seem to matter, however, for Jamaicans in Toronto where the proportion of Jamaicans with university degrees in a neighborhood is negatively associated with residential concentration, net of covariates (Model IV, Table 7.2). The proportion foreign-born shows a significant positive effect on residential concentration in New York and this does not appear to be any different for the other two areas, although the line for Toronto in Figure 7.5, shows a fairly flat line, arguing that while not a statistically significant difference, there may be something different about the effect of acculturation on Jamaicans in Toronto. While self-employment did not result in a statistically significant effect in the regression model, we can see from Figure 7.6 that the line for Miami contrasts with the flatter slopes for New York and Toronto. Model IV explains about 58 per cent of the variation in the residential patterns of Jamaicans.

In contrast to the Chinese in New York, socioeconomic resources are not associated with residential integration for New York Jamaicans. Those in Miami are more likely to follow a path of assimilation as well as those in Toronto. Acculturation, on the other hand, does have an integrating effect for Jamaicans in all areas, although the effect is much less in Toronto, where the flatter slope suggests a pattern of ethnic retention. For Jamaicans then, there is evidence to suggest that this group follows a general path of residential dispersion but cross-metropolitan differences suggest that it also depends on the social context.

Table 7.2 Regression of logit proportion Jamaican on group characteristics and metropolitan area

Jamaicans	Model 1	Model 2	Model 3	Model 4
Metropolitan area (NY omitted)	-	-	-	-
Miami	-.031	-,276	-.265 *	.339
Toronto	-.777 **	-.013	-.895 **	.018
Proportion univ. degree	.023	-	-	-.132
Degree*Miami	-1.936 **	-	-	-.787
Degree*Toronto	-2.044 **	-	-	-1.487 **
Proportion foreign	-	1.504 **	-	1.040 **
Foreign*Miami	-	-.069	-	-.443
Foreign*Toronto	-	-1.177 **	-	-.857
Proportion self-employed	-	-	.132	-.589
Self*Miami	-	-	-.658	1.630
Self*Toronto	-	-	-1.813	.799
Tract size (logged)				-.644 **
Constant	-1.750 **	-2.880 **	-1.753 **	2.891 **
Adjust R^2	.450 **	.430 **	.420 **	.580 **
N		519		

*p<.1; ** p<.05

Figure 7.4 Net effect of proportion university degree on proportion Jamaican in census tracts

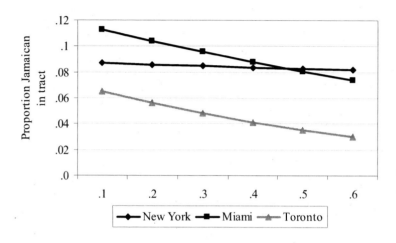

Figure 7.5 Net effect of proportion foreign-born on proportion Jamaican in census tracts

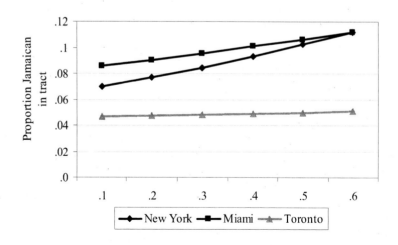

Figure 7.6 Net effect of proportion self-employed on proportion Jamaican in census tracts

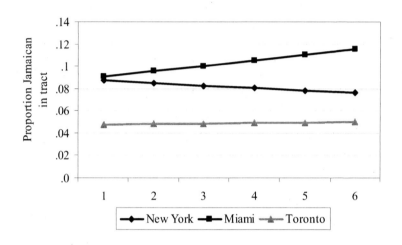

Iranians

The same models are repeated for Iranian tracts pooled across three metropolitan areas, Los Angeles, Toronto and Vancouver, and omitted for San Francisco. These results are shown in Table 7.3. The coefficient for the proportion Iranian with a university degree, isolated in Model I, shows that, though negative, it has no significant association with residential patterns in Los Angeles (likely as a result of the small sample size). Although the statistical results suggest that the effect of education does not depend on the metropolitan area, the positive coefficients for Toronto and Vancouver indicate that socioeconomic resources, as measured by educational attainment, may actually have a segregating effect.

Model II also shows that Iranian residential integration is not affected by the proportion of foreign-born Iranians in a neighborhood in Los Angeles. However, this does not hold for Toronto, where this indicator of acculturation leads to the residential dispersion of Iranians. That is, as the proportion foreign-born of the ethnic group increases in a tract, the co-ethnic concentration also increases. Thus, as the proportion of foreign-born decreases, there are also less co-ethnic members. While the coefficient for Vancouver Iranians did not emerge as statistically different from L.A. (Vancouver Iranians n=27), its magnitude suggests that it is not much different from Toronto.

The association between self-employment and residential integration depends on the metropolitan area as revealed in Model III, Table 7.3. In Los Angeles, self-employment leads to residential concentration and this appears to be even more evident in Vancouver. But in Toronto, it is associated with residential integration demonstrating the influence of the urban context on Iranian integration.

When all variables are included in the model, the effect of education remains negative and not statistically significant, despite having a larger coefficient, and the differences between L.A. and the two Canadian metropolitan areas are reduced. The slightly greater integrating effect of education for Iranians in L.A. can be observed when comparing the three lines in Figure 7.7 in its slightly steeper slope. Model IV in Table 7.3 also shows that net of covariates, the proportion of foreign-born Iranians is positively associated with proportion Iranian in neighborhoods despite the lack of statistical significance. The magnitude of the interaction terms for Toronto and Vancouver are reduced in the expanded model but does not appear to be significantly different from L.A.

The greater concentrating effect of the proportion foreign-born in the two Canadian metros is visible in Figure 7.8, which indicates that acculturation has a dispersing effect on Iranians. The effect of the third ethnic resource variable, self-employment, continues to be dependent on the metropolitan area, holding the other variables constant, and this is shown in the graph in Figure 7.9 These three variables, with their interactions, along with the tract size accounts for 45 per cent of the variation in logit proportion Iranian in neighborhoods.

The statistical tests do not present significant results by metropolitan area for Iranians indicating a common pattern of ethnic retention with respect to the effect of socioeconomic resources and acculturation. However, the gap in the lines in Figures 7.7 and 7.8 suggest that there may be some important distinctions between Iranians in those metropolitan areas. This goes against predictions of assimilation for White ethnic groups we specified in Chapter Two. Yet, it does support the hypothesis regarding the group-specific context of migration. The primarily involuntary nature of migration for many Iranians has lead to a more cohesive residential community.

Table 7.3 OLS regression of logit proportion Iranians on group characteristics and metropolitan area

Iranian	Model 1	Model 2	Model 3	Model 4
Metropolitan area (L.A. omitted)	-	-		-
Toronto	-.955 **	-2.708 **	-.295	-1.758
Vancouver	-1.049 **	-3.254 **	-1.083 **	-2.610 *
Proportion univ. degree	-.198	-	-	-.620
Degree*Toronto	.559	-	-	.370
Degree*Vancouver	.457	-	-	-.080
Proportion foreign	-	.010	-	.301
Foreign*Toronto	-	2.279 *	-	1.458
Foreign*Vancouver	-	2.720	-	1.836
Proportion self-employed	-	-	1.189 **	1.173 *
Self*Toronto	-	-	-1.620	-1.376
Self*Vancouver	-	-	3.074 *	3.288 *
Tract size (logged)				-.445 **
Constant	-2.007 **	-2.103 **	-2.451 **	1.410
Adjust R^2	.330 **	.370 **	.390 **	.450 **
N			116	

*p<.1; ** p<.05

Figure 7.7 Net effect of proportion university degree on proportion Iranian in census tracts

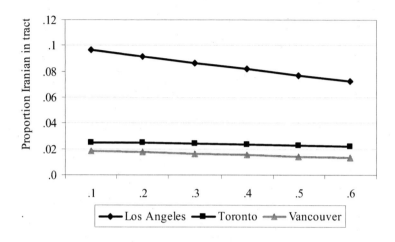

Figure 7.8 Net effect of proportion foreign-born on proportion Iranian in census tracts

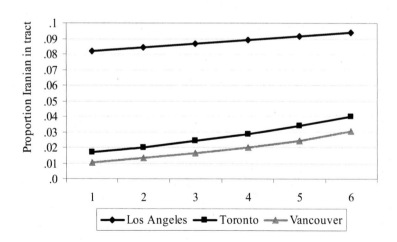

Figure 7.9 Net effect of proportion self-employed on proportion Iranian in census tracts

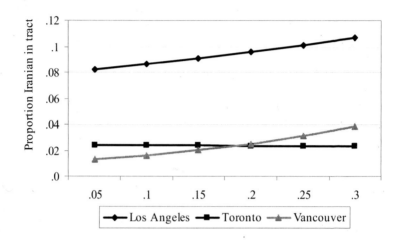

Vietnamese

For the three metropolitan areas with available tract level data on Vietnamese characteristics – Los Angeles, San Francisco and Toronto – educational attainment is negatively associated with the logit of proportion Vietnamese in a tract. This occurs for L.A. as well as for the other two metros (Model I, Table 7.4). Again, due to insufficient data, the analysis omits neighborhoods in Montréal.

In Model II, no metropolitan interaction effect is observed in the results for proportion foreign-born. For all areas, a higher proportion of foreign-born Vietnamese in a neighborhood is associated with a higher logit of proportion Vietnamese in that neighborhood. Although positive, the effect of foreign-born is not statistically significant with the pooled sample used in the model.

Model III also shows no statistically significant association between the proportion of self-employed Vietnamese in a neighborhood with the logit of proportion Vietnamese as well as no statistically significant interaction terms, which is indicative of similar metropolitan effects.

However, the coefficients in the third column of values in Table 7.4 show a difference in the direction of the effect, especially for Toronto.

The final column in the table reveals that the significant effect of education for the Vietnamese in Los Angeles is not reduced with the inclusion of the other two ethnic resource variables or by controlling tract size. It shows that education continues to have an integrating effect in L.A. and that less gains are made in San Francisco and Toronto. The relatively flat lines in Figure 7.10 for the two latter areas reveal more of a pattern of retention, suggesting that the statistical tests may be misleading of some interesting patterns since the gains of education in residential integration for those in L.A. is much greater than the gains observed for the Vietnamese in the other two places. The residential integration of the Vietnamese in San Francisco and Toronto also appear to be more sensitive to acculturation, where the positive slopes suggest a pattern of concentration with an increasing foreign-born proportion, despite the statistical results (Figure 7.11). Akin to the other ethnic groups, the effect of self-employment is not consistent across the represented metropolitan areas for the Vietnamese; a positive effect is observed in L.A., no effect is observed in San Francisco, and a slight negative effect is observed in Toronto. This expanded model explains about the same level of variation as the model does for the Chinese, 23 per cent.

No great statistical difference is found in the effects of the three dimensions of ethnic resources by metropolitan area but some differences are observed which suggest that, like Jamaicans, the integration patterns of the Vietnamese may be affected by the social context. I find a tendency for residential dispersion in Los Angeles and for retention in San Francisco and Toronto. This suggests that the context of migration may be important for the Vietnamese in these two latter places but less so in L.A.

Table 7.4 OLS regression of logit proportion Vietnamese on group characteristics and metropolitan area

Vietnamese	Model 1	Model 2	Model 3	Model 4
Metropolitan area (L.A. omitted)	-	-	-	-
San Francisco	-.068	.738	.112	-.245
Toronto	-.988 **	-1.091	-.841 **	-1.511
Proportion univ. degree	-1.057 *	-	-	-1.541 **
Degree*San Francisco	.812	-	-	1.384
Degree*Toronto	-.328	-	-	1.361
Proportion foreign	-	1.293	-	.381
Foreign*San Francisco	-	-.866	-	.213
Foreign*Toronto	-	.333	-	.735
Proportion self-employed	-	-	.601	1.232
Self*San Francisco	-	-	-.643	-1.052
Self*Toronto	-	-	-1.209	-2.069
Tract size (logged)	-	-	-	-.783 **
Constant	-1.759 **	-2.942 **	-1.983 **	4.675 **
Adjust R^2	.160 **	.160 **	.150 **	.230 **
N		266		

*p<.1; ** p<.05

Figure 7.10 Net effect of proportion university degree on proportion Vietnamese in census tracts

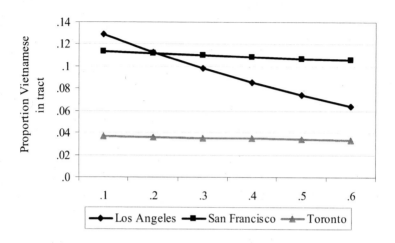

Figure 7.11 Net effect of proportion foreign-born on proportion Vietnamese in census tracts

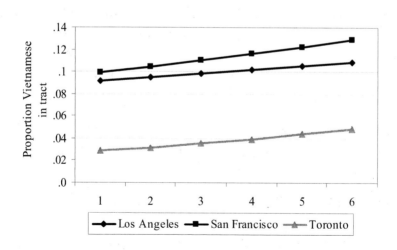

Figure 7.12 Net effect of proportion self-employed on proportion Vietnamese in census tracts

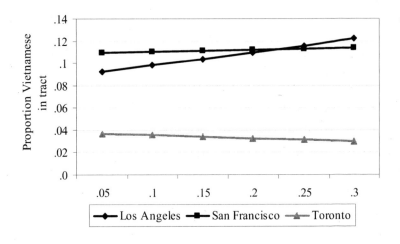

METROPOLITAN VARIATION IN ETHNIC PATHWAYS

The analysis of four ethnic groups finds both ethnic variation in integration patterns and metropolitan variation. As evidence of metropolitan variation, the same ethnic groups in different metropolitan areas (and countries) do not always experience the same process of residential integration. For instance, the degree of residential concentration is not similarly affected by ethnic resources across metropolitan areas, most especially for Jamaicans and Vietnamese. Jamaicans appear to undergo a process of spatial assimilation most evidently in Miami and to some extent in Toronto but not in New York. The Vietnamese in San Francisco and Toronto also present evidence of ethnic retention on both socioeconomic and acculturation indicators but this does not occur in Los Angeles.

The Chinese are the most likely to consistently follow the pattern predicted by the spatial assimilation model in the four metropolitan areas across the two countries. This suggests that regardless of urban and national contexts, the Chinese have a tendency to prefer residential dispersal with increasing exposure and socioeconomic resources and that residential proximity, for the most part, is not a central feature of their ethnic identity and community. This is not to suggest that there are not pockets of Chinese neighborhoods in the suburbs but that the general pattern appears to be assimilation.

Iranians as well seem less inclined to be affected by urban and national contexts. While they show some weak signs of residential dispersal with socioeconomic mobility and acculturation, none of these coefficients are statistically significant. The empirical evidence reveals a tendency for ethnic residential distinctiveness. They do not seem to move away from one another with rising ethnic resources, especially in Los Angeles but also in the two Canadian metropolitan areas. This suggests that Chinese and Iranian residential integration is less affected by the social context and more affected by group-related factors such as cultural and social ties and the context of migration.

Further evidence of metropolitan variation in residential patterns arose with self-employment. The effect of self-employment is not clearly in one direction or another for any of the groups. In essence, it appears that this resource is more linked to the urban context leading to residential dispersion in some places and to residential concentration in other places for the same group.

In studies of residential segregation, metropolitan variation in neighborhood residential integration is often attributed to differences in urban ecology, which recognizes that distinctive local characteristics shape where and how social groups sort and settle across neighborhoods. The ecological framework argues that the spatial differentiation of ethnic groups is a reflection of urban social organization (Park, Burgess, McKenzie 1925). Group relations do not form in isolation from the urban structure and environment but are shaped through the opportunities and constraints that have shaped the city over time. Metropolitan areas develop in unique ways and are affected by social, political and economic forces that structure the residential location of its residents. The ecological model highlights key factors such as population size and composition, urban economy and housing construction, and migration flows for influencing residential patterns within metropolitan areas (Farley and Frey 1994; Fong 1996; Frey and Farley 1996; Logan, Stults and Farley 2004; Massey and Denton 1987; White, Fong and Cai 2003; White and Glick 1999).

Table 7.5 Selected characteristics of metropolitan areas in the U.S. and Canada, proportions

	U.S.				Canada		
	New York	L.A.	San Francisco	Miami	Toronto	Montréal	Vancouver
Population size	21,199,865	16,373,645	7,039,362	3,876,380	4,682,897	3,380,645	1,967,475
White	.56	.39	.50	.36	.65	.89	.65
Black	.16	.07	.07	.19	.07	.04	.01
Latino	.18	.40	.20	.40	.02	.02	.01
Asian	.07	.10	.18	.02	.24	.05	.33
New housing	.07	.11	.11	.17	.15	.10	.23
Foreign-born	.24	.31	.27	.40	.43	.19	.39

Note: All Consolidated Metropolitan Statistical Areas in the U.S., Census Metropolitan Areas in Canada.

As we saw in the foregoing analysis, the degree of ethnic residential concentration and the processes of ethnic integration can vary by metropolitan area. Table 7.5 lists the factors that may contribute to variation in residential patterns across urban areas for a given ethnic group. Jamaicans and the Chinese in the New York CMSA are living in the most populous metropolitan area in North America, where over half of the population are White. New York also has a high proportion of Blacks (.16) relative to the six other metros and less than one in ten Asians. Compared with all other metros, the housing stock tends to be older with the lowest rate of new housing construction (during the 10 years prior to the census). Surprisingly, New York also has one of the lowest proportion foreign-born of all the included areas.

Iranians and the Vietnamese who are in the Los Angeles CMSA are also living in a large metropolitan area. At a population of 16 million, it is the second largest conurbation in North America but quite different in its composition to New York. In contrast to the New York CMSA, L.A. is less White, less Black and more Latino and Asian. Approximately one in ten homes were built in the 1990s and one in three people are foreign-born. Chinese, Iranian and Vietnamese residents in the San Francisco CMSA are also living in a somewhat distinctive place. Like L.A., the two largest proportions of non-White groups are Latinos and Asians and the construction of new homes is similar but San Francisco has a greater proportion of Whites, a lower proportion foreign-born and is less populated. The fourth U.S. metropolitan area included for Jamaicans, i.e. Miami, stands out for its relatively high proportions of Blacks and Latinos and small population. Whites only comprise about 36 per cent of the CMSA and Asians, 2 per cent. Even more than the three other U.S. metros, Miami is an immigrant destination, with 40 per cent foreign-born.

The three metropolitan areas in Canada are striking for their contrasts in composition from places in the U.S. All four groups in the Toronto CMA confront a racial composition quite different from their counterparts in U.S. metropolitan areas. Almost two thirds of Toronto residents are White and about one quarter are Asian. Fifteen per cent of homes have been constructed in the 1990s and Toronto houses the largest foreign-born proportion of all seven represented metros. Iranians and Chinese communities in the Vancouver CMA are not in a vastly different urban racial mix as those in Toronto but there are much more Asians and less of other racial minorities in this West Coast metro.

Vancouver is also a newer metropolitan area, with about one quarter of newly constructed homes. While there are some similarities between Toronto and Vancouver, Jamaicans and Vietnamese in Montréal are situated in a different urban context. One that is largely White and non-immigrant.

This comparison of metropolitan areas shows that these conurbations are highly distinctive in their attributes as they have developed in particular ways, shaped differently by the forces of migration and urban development and planning. We also notice cross-national patterns, most especially in the racial composition as well as in population size. There appears to be more racial diversity in the U.S. context and U.S. CMSAs tend to be larger. Given these structural differences, ethnic residential processes outcomes cannot be expected to be uniform, even for those groups that share an ethnic heritage. Nevertheless, there is some evidence of this, with variation by ethnic group.

SUMMARY AND DISCUSSION

This chapter began with the question of ethnic, metropolitan and national differences in the processes of residential integration for groups in Canada and the United States. The results of the empirical analysis for the Chinese, Jamaicans, Iranians and Vietnamese in various places lend support for viewing ethnic integration in comparative terms.

For particular groups, such as the Jamaicans and the Vietnamese, the social context plays an important role for understanding their residential processes. Others, such as the Chinese and Iranians, appear to be somewhat resilient to the social context in terms of the effect of socioeconomic resources and acculturation on residential concentration. The relationship between self-employment and residential concentration for all groups, however, is clearly linked to the urban context.

The Chinese, an Asian ethnic group, provided evidence in partial support of what was expected in U.S. metropolitan areas. As expected, a path of spatial assimilation was supported for this ethnic group in Los Angeles and San Francisco. However, where we expected to find ethnic retention operating for comparable groups in Canadian metropolitan areas, notably Toronto and Vancouver, this did not surface. Instead, the Chinese were consistent in their tendency for residential dispersion with increasing cultural adaptation and socioeconomic resources.

These results are also consistent with other studies on Chinese residential patterns in particular metropolitan areas. Although not a comparative study, Zhou and Logan's (1991) study of the New York Chinese showed that residential mobility was associated with socioeconomic mobility. Moreover, a recent study on the Chinese in Toronto revealed that language assimilation (i.e. acculturation) was associated with leaving the ethnic neighborhood (Myles and Hou 2004). However, income only had a modest effect. The current findings support these other studies and expand our understanding of Chinese residential distinctiveness in other places.

The context of migration is especially helpful for understanding Chinese integration patterns in various places. As elucidated in Chapter Six, the Chinese have a long history in both countries as economic migrants. Due to their expectations for economic success and mobility, I argued that economic migrants would be more likely to follow the path of spatial assimilation. This was confirmed for the Chinese.

Jamaicans form another ethnic group that arrived in both countries to seek better economic opportunities. As predicted by this context of migration, one that promotes the selectivity of migrants (Chiswick 1982), Jamaicans in Toronto and Miami adhere to a pattern of spatial assimilation or residential dispersion with acculturation and economic mobility. This has been supported elsewhere, at least in Toronto (Myles and Hou 2004). However, those in New York appear to be a special case.

Past studies on Jamaicans, or more broadly, West Indians, in New York can shed some light on this discrepancy. Jamaican integration in New York occurs in a setting with a large native-born and residentially segregated Black population (Foner 1998). While there is a large proportion of Blacks in Miami, they are outweighed by the presence of Latinos, the largest ethnic minority group (Table 7.5). And in Toronto, Asians are the most dominant minority presence. In New York then, Jamaican immigrants are faced with a racially-heightened context of assimilation and find themselves maintaining their distinctiveness within this environment (Crowder and Tedrow 2001). The stronger sense of a Jamaican national identity in New York compared to Canada also supports this explanation (Thompson and Bauer 2003).

Iranians, in contrast to the Chinese and Jamaicans, arrived in a different context of migration and reception. Although they are a White ethnic group, they are distinctive from European groups in their religious and linguistic composition, and in their specific context of migration and reception. As discussed previously, they are comprised largely of refugees and for this reason, it is not surprising that their ethnic solidarity is manifested in urban space. They are a highly concentrated group in residential terms, especially in Los Angeles, and the proportions of Iranians in the neighborhoods of the three metropolitan areas do not diminish when the proportion of university educated Iranians increase, although there is slight evidence of integration with acculturation.

This is also supported by previous work on Iranians that argued that despite the high levels of acculturation and socioeconomic status, the mindset of Iranian immigrants supports a cohesive Iranian community (Hoffman 1989; Modarresi 2001; Mostofi 2003). They are one of the most highly educated ethnic groups in the U.S. and Canada. In terms of this study, they are the most educated of the four ethnic groups in this analysis and second in line out of the fourteen groups in the earlier analysis, second to Asian/East Indians in the U.S. and to Koreans in Canada (Appendix A). In addition, high levels of English language acquisition is also evident, at least in the United Sates (Hoffman 1989; Modarresi 2001). But the initial mindset of Iranian migrants to the U.S. that perceived of their stay as temporary has evolved into an acceptance of the long-term basis of their movement. This awareness and the emotional and familial attachment to Iran, along with increased numbers of Iranians in places like Los Angeles, contribute to a desire to preserve Iranian culture, language and community (Modaressi 2001). Moreover, as Hoffman (1989) argues, it is erroneous to assume that linguistic assimilation is concomitant to the erosion of an ethnic culture, which for Iranians, is evidently linked to residential proximity.

Like Iranians, the Vietnamese also arrived in large numbers to Canada and the United States, in the context of war. Given the mostly involuntary nature of migration, we would expect them to be more likely to preserve their connection to one another and their home country. This is observed in their residential patterns for Toronto and San Francisco. However, in contrast to Iranians, the Vietnamese were greeted in a relatively warmer political climate, which should be expected to foster residential dispersion and this is shown by the data for Los Angeles, in the effect of education. The varying pattern of residential incorporation across metropolitan areas suggests that this group is more likely to be affected by the urban context.

Studies examining Vietnamese integration point to the importance of the family (Kibria 1994; Killian and Hegtvedt 2003; Zhou and

Bankston 1994) and community (Zhou and Bankston 1994) in adaptation processes. Many Vietnamese immigrants face barriers in the labor market and low economic status (Lamba 2003; Valtonen 2004; Zhou and Bankston 1994) but have used family and community strategies to exit from disadvantaged conditions. In particular, these ethnic institutions, along with the church, promote values that encourage the educational and occupational attainment of their second generation so that they become part of mainstream middle-class America. On the other hand, these same institutions also ensure the continuation of the Vietnamese culture and community. Such strong ties within the Vietnamese community can explain the lack of residential dispersion evident in the data although this is less so in Los Angeles, where the largest Vietnamese community resides.

As this discussion reveals, the increasing diversity of North American cities brings about a distinct challenge in studies of ethnic integration. The challenge lies in balancing the interest in making generalized statements about the integration process with the particularities of ethnic groups and their experiences. Much of the evidence in the era of the new immigration argues for group-specific analysis since race, religion, socio-political factors and community dynamics all affect integration patterns and groups vary substantially along these lines.

In support of the growing literature on ethnic communities, this study uses residential concentration as one indicator of integration to make three key points. First, there are ethnic effects on residential integration. Ethnic groups adapt to metropolitan conditions using the social, cultural and economic strategies available to them, demonstrating that different groups in the same place will behave differently. Part of this explanation appears to be related to the context of migration. We find that groups that are comprised of large refugee populations tend to maintain their levels of concentration. In contrast, groups that migrated for primarily economic reasons find themselves more likely to disperse.

Second, there are metropolitan effects on residential integration. The same ethnic group adapts in particular ways to different metropolitan contexts. While the social, cultural and economic strategies may be similar due to the same ethnic origin, the conditions under which these strategies are being employed differ and will result in different outcomes. The patterns observed for Jamaicans and Vietnamese offer two examples of this.

Third, there are cross-national effects on residential integration. In general, the four ethnic groups in the Canadian metropolitan areas that were included in the analysis were less concentrated than their counterparts in the U.S., net of group resources. This is likely the result of the relatively smaller proportions of these selected ethnic groups in the metropolitan areas of Canada than in U.S. areas. Despite these differences, no systematic cross-national pattern emerged in ethnic residential processes. Ethnic groups in Canadian metropolitan areas were not more likely to use resources to maintain their residential distinctiveness as their counterparts in the United States.

These key points are based upon an empirical analysis with data limitations suggesting that we may be getting a partial story for the ethnic groups in the study. However, even with fuller data for groups in Canada we find similar patterns with very slight differences (see Appendix C). As expected, groups are less concentrated with the fuller dataset but the overall conclusions regarding their residential integration remain much the same. The data used for this analysis, although restricted, still reveal important ethnic, metropolitan and (to some extent) national differences in residential concentration for four ethnic groups in Canada and the United States. These differences highlight the ethnic character of residential concentration, an indicator of integration, as well as the importance of the context of migration and the local environment.

CHAPTER EIGHT

Conclusions:
Ethnic integration in comparative perspective

The ethnic integration process is embedded in a larger institutional and ideological milieu and this has implications for residential patterns. The comparative analysis of ethnic residential integration in Canada and the United States presented here reveals that there are important cross-national differences. The cross-national differences that emerged, however, were not consistent across all ethnic groups thus underscoring the importance of ethnicity and ethnic boundaries in the study of integration and its processes. This final chapter reviews findings from the bi-level analysis and addresses their implications for the pathways to residential incorporation, our understanding of the two host societies, and for ethnic incorporation more generally.

I began this endeavor with several expectations regarding cross-national differences in ethnic residential integration that were based on five dimensions of the national context in Canada and the United States; immigration policy, settlement programs, structure of inequality, housing context and integration ideology and policies. The differences found were not always in the directions predicted but they are nonetheless important and reveal some significant patterns.

First, not all ethnic groups were consistently more likely to have higher levels of segregation in the U.S. versus Canada or *vice versa*. The patterns varied by ethnic group and by measurement. According to the Dissimilarity Index, Germans, Italians, Filipinos, Vietnamese, Koreans and Pakistanis were more segregated in the urban areas of Canada than in the U.S., Iranians, Jamaicans, and Haitians were more segregated in the U.S. than in Canada, and there were no differences in levels between English, Polish, Russians, Chinese and Asian/East Indians across the two countries.

Yet, whether the patterns between the two countries are due to the national context or whether they are the consequence of compositional differences of a given group that developed out of varied migration histories and differential streams to the two countries is unclear. As a result, other factors such as the degree of acculturation, socioeconomic resources, group size, self-employment, the metropolitan and regional context were controlled in the multivariate analysis.

To summarize the multivariate results, White ethnic groups, overall, were not more likely to follow the path of spatial assimilation in the U.S. than in Canada, at the metropolitan level. Their paths and their levels of residential concentration were roughly similar using both the Index of Dissimilarity and the Isolation Index. Black ethnic groups, overall, were not more likely to be follow the path predicted by place stratification in the U.S. compared to Canada. As with White groups, the paths were strikingly similar. However, Black groups in the U.S. were more residentially segregated than in Canada. And finally, patterns for Asian ethnic groups were more nuanced. Acculturation had a greater assimilating effect on Asian groups in the U.S. than on Asian groups in Canada, but socioeconomic resources had the opposite impact. Socioeconomic resources had a greater assimilating effect on Asian groups in Canada than on comparable groups in the U.S. However, metropolitan segregation levels for Asian groups in the U.S. were generally lower than in Canada.

These results are somewhat consistent with past comparative work on segregation levels between Canada and the U.S., which showed that there were small differences between the two countries (Johnston et al. 2007b; Peach 2005; White, Fong and Cai 2003). Where there were differences, groups tended to have lower levels of segregation in Canada with the exception of Blacks.

Despite the lack of support for the hypotheses set out at the beginning, one model for U.S. panethnic groups in the United States emerged. All three groups were characterized by negative associations between acculturation and residential segregation and positive associations between socioeconomic status and segregation. In other words, acculturation is likely to lead to residential dispersion but not socioeconomic status. Canadian panethnic groups did not consistently follow one model of incorporation but revealed three different models. In one model, acculturation has an integrating effect but not SES, such as for White ethnic groups. In a second model, socioeconomic status has an integrating effect but not acculturation, such as for Asian ethnic groups.

The third model, which is evident of a place stratification effect, applies to Black ethnic groups in Canada.

In this broader level of analysis across all metropolitan areas, we observed urban structural effects as well. This was further supported by the investigation of four ethnic groups, Chinese, Jamaican, Iranian and Vietnamese, in specific metropolitan areas of the United States and Canada, which demonstrated how the urban context can also lead to divergent processes and outcomes for ethnic integration. However, this was not the case for all groups. Rather, there appeared to be more of a consistent pattern of residential incorporation processes across metropolitan areas and national borders for the same ethnic group. For example, Chinese and Jamaicans were more likely to disperse from ethnic neighborhoods with increasing acculturation and socioeconomic resources in most of the metropolitan areas studied. In contrast, Vietnamese and Iranians revealed a tendency toward retaining ethnic distinctiveness with rising acculturation and socioeconomic resources in the majority of areas included in the analysis.

IMPLICATIONS FOR PATHWAYS TO RESIDENTIAL INCORPORATION

The higher levels of segregation for particular groups, i.e. Asian groups in Canada, Black groups in the U.S., suggest that these groups will likely maintain their identity and culture for some time given the link between spatial and social distinctiveness (Peach 2005). In addition to examining segregation levels to gain insight into intra- and inter-group relations, pathways to residential incorporation also provide a window on a group's tendency (or not) toward integration to the mainstream and provide more in-depth understanding of differences between countries.

The results from the data analyses confirm that there is no universal pathway to residential incorporation. The age-old prediction of spatial assimilation or ethnic residential dispersion is, once again, only partially supported. But even the partial support does not fall in the expected direction. Contrary to expectations, Asian and White – mostly European – ethnic groups in the United States did not demonstrate a clear and obvious tendency towards residential dispersion. Iranians, counted as a White ethnic group, also did not appear to take this expected path, although there was evidence that the Chinese in the larger metropolitan areas of the two countries may be residentially assimilating.

What is readily apparent in the results is that many panethnic and ethnic groups remain residentially distinctive in the metropolitan areas of both countries and may actually use socioeconomic resources to achieve a more spatially cohesive ethnic community. This is not surprising given the emergence and persistence of middle-class ethnic neighborhoods and "ethnoburbs" in metropolitan areas (Crowder and Tedrow 2001; Lacy 2004; Li 1998; Zhou and Logan 1991; Modarres 1992). The high levels of income and education with which many recent waves of migrants have come partly explain this association. Socioeconomic status may now have less to do with equal access to neighborhoods than it once did and more to do with groups seeking residential concentration.

While SES may not be the answer to ethnic residential integration between panethnic groups, acculturation is more promising as a determinant of declining residential concentration. This was evident particularly in the U.S. context, and to some degree in Canada. One national pattern for the U.S. emerged and applied to all three panethnic groupings. Whether the pattern can be explained by the same process is open to question, and given what we know about residential sorting processes in the U.S. case, particularly for racialized groups, a universal U.S. integration pathway is highly unlikely even if the patterns appear similar.

In Canada, residential processes are more clearly distinct for each panethnic grouping, with some evidence of spatial assimilation for White and Asian ethnic groups and evidence of place stratification and retention in the Black groups. Interestingly, Black groups in Canada were less likely to exhibit tendencies toward residential assimilation than Black groups in the U.S.

The lack of evidence of spatial assimilation processes at the broader level of analysis with the more encompassing ethnic boundaries suggests that this may not be the level we should be studying to understand processes of ethnic residential incorporation. In addition, the cross-sectional nature of the data precludes us from making causal claims about the associations found in the statistical analyses. The data then, are also a limiting factor for making conclusive statements about residential incorporation processes over time. However, the panethnic patterns we observed do provide a general picture of segregation across the two countries. This level of analysis has been useful for comparing levels of residential segregation across countries by panethnic grouping and for showing some cross-national patterns, but by masking important variations by ethnic origin or ancestry it has been less useful for providing insight into residential processes than the investigation of ethnic groups in particular places.

There is evidence of spatial assimilation when specific ethnic groups in specific metropolitan areas are examined. Although the effect of the national context is less clear due to metropolitan factors, one line of differentiation clearly emerges. Two of the ethnic groups, which are of different linguistic, phenotypic and cultural backgrounds, revealed a pattern of integration that reflects residential dispersion. Their common link? Both ethnic groups, Chinese and Jamaicans, share economic motivations for migrating to Canada and the United States. The two other groups, also of different linguistic, phenotypic and cultural backgrounds, revealed a similar path of ethnic residential *retention*. Many members of these groups, Vietnamese and Iranians, left war-torn places involuntarily and had to create new homes in foreign places. Given the context of these migrations, it can only be expected that these groups will turn to their ethnic communities for comfort and understanding, and feel a need to preserve their ethnic heritage. For these groups, their ethnic cohesiveness is manifested spatially and supported by cultures that value ethnic linkages.

Based on this level of analysis, we are able to better identify the context under which ethnic groups residentially concentrate or disperse. However, given the limited number of metropolitan areas it is difficult to know whether these patterns are specific to large metropolitan areas with large concentrations of ethnic group members. Panethnic patterns are also indiscernible. These limitations in the more restricted examination are addressed by the broader level of analysis. The inherent value of the bi-level analysis is demonstrated in complementary nature of the findings. Without one or the other, we would have a more limited view of ethnic integration in the United States and Canada.

With respect to the on-going debate that questions the theoretical relevance of the three residential integration perspectives, this study provides one response. There is sufficient evidence to show spatial assimilation, place stratification and ethnic retention take place in the urban areas of each country, with variation according to ethnic group, the level of ethnic detail, the urban structure, the choice of segregation measure and the type of ethnic resource. However, where spatial assimilation is clearly in evidence or not in the empirical results, it proved more challenging to differentiate between place stratification and ethnic retention processes.

In reality, research on residential preferences suggests an interaction of in-group tendencies and social distance are likely to be part of the explanation for persistent concentration, although racial stratification may be more likely to operate on U.S. patterns (Adelman 2005; Charles 2003; Fong 1994; Krysan and Farley 2002; Pattillo 2005). The extent to which persistent segregation is the result of in-group preferences or out-group avoidance is an area for further clarification, especially in Canada.

Based on the experiences of ethnic groups in this study, it makes sense to reformulate our theoretical understanding of immigrant and ethnic residential concentration. Rather than two conceptually distinct perspectives, a synthesis of place stratification and ethnic retention is key to understanding persistent residential distinctiveness. Immigrant and ethnic groups are faced with a structure that is not of their own construction but are able to navigate within this structure in a way that makes sense to them. West Indians in New York provide one example of a group that has maintained a sense of ethnic identity and ethnic space within a racial structure that pools them among native-born Blacks (Crowder and Tedrow 2001). Lacy (2004) refers to this as "strategic assimilation." Place stratification can be helpful for understanding the concentration of poverty in segregated neighborhoods but appears to be growing less helpful for understanding persistent concentration at higher levels of socioeconomic status where ethnic groups members have the resources to better control their residential movement.

On the other hand, the ethnic retention perspective, by focusing on in-group preferences neglects the wider racial and ethnic context in which these preferences are manifested. Many ethnic groups continue to have the perception of being not fully accepted by mainstream society, in both countries. The difficulty in disentangling the degree to which in-group preferences emerge as a result of out-group hostility, has not yet been addressed. As a result, a merging of these perspectives is needed.

THE NATIONAL CONTEXT

Five dimensions of the national context were identified as having some importance in explaining cross-national differences in the residential integration of ethnic groups; immigration policy, institutionalization of settlement services, structure of inequality, the housing context, and integration policy and ideology. The first four were expected to lead to the residential concentration of ethnic groups in the U.S. but dispersion in Canada. Integration policy and ideology was expected to lead to residential dispersion in the U.S. but concentration in Canada.

Many of the contextual factors identified at the national level did not produce the expected cross-national pattern in residential incorporation processes. Rather, what is striking is the lack of the direct effect of much of the national institutional context. This is not surprising with respect to the immigration policy, as Reitz (1998) has pointed out previously. Differences in the institutionalization of the settlement sector also did not appear to lead to large differences in residential processes suggesting that this aspect is likely to be more prominent for new arrivals and for particular groups in particular places as shown in the work by Bloemraad (2003). The housing context is also not a clear distinguishing factor in the explanation of urban residential patterns across countries. Finally, there is evidence to show that the mosaic and melting pot contrast may be relegated to the past. This has been supported also in the work of Peach (2005), who found little difference in the segregation levels of non-Blacks across the U.S. and Canada, leading him to conclude that this aspect of the national context had negligible impact on residential processes. However, rather than having little impact, it may be more plausible that both countries, in dealing with the new immigration, have adopted some degree of official pluralist discourse and are simultaneously grappling with maintaining a unifying identity. Thus, in terms of the ideology of integration, the two countries may be converging; either that, or its effect on integration is overrated (Harles 2004).

There is one key national factor to emerge in this study of ethnic residential segregation, and that is the structure of inequality, or more specifically, the racial or ethnic structure of host societies. Other dimensions, while important, are likely to be mediated by this aspect of the two countries. The somewhat dissimilar patterns of panethnic and ethnic integration across borders suggests that a structural condition that provides differential opportunities to groups within a host society is key to understanding these patterns. The contextual dimension implicated in these findings is the structure of racial and ethnic inequality more so than any of the other aspects of the institutional context. In terms of the residential integration process, ethnic groups are faced with a unique racial or ethnic structure in which residential decisions are made and the degree of concentration is likely to be a form of adjustment to local and national conditions and attitudes about race relations that either encourage or discourage clustering for a given group.

The greater level of segregation of Black ethnic groups in the U.S. compared to Canada demonstrates that they continue to have fewer opportunities to residentially integrate in the former than in the latter. And studies on racial stratification show that these restrictions to residential mobility is more likely to be operating on U.S. patterns for Black groups (Adelman 2005; Charles 2003; Fong 1994; Krysan and Farley 2002; Pattillo 2005).

The greater concentration of Asian ethnic groups in Canada raises an interesting question with respect to the racial structure in Canada. As the largest non-White panethnic group, their integration will be key to understanding ethnic and racial relations in that country. Our understanding of the two contexts imply that residential dispersion is more likely to be encouraged in Asian groups in the United States compared to those in Canada. Asian groups in Canada are likely to be asserting their ethnicity in an institutional context that supports ethnic distinctiveness. However, further research is needed to verify whether this has, in fact, occurred.

The lack of a clear direct effect of the national context suggests that much of the institutional differences across countries operate through more localized processes. This points to the value of examining local variations in institutional structures, which are also shaped by forces at the national level. Future research should continue to focus on these local structures and examine the impact of the institutional context at this level, keeping in mind that local structures are set within a national context.

IMPLICATIONS FOR STUDIES OF ETHNIC INTEGRATION

These results also have three main implications for studies of ethnic integration in general. First, they show that acculturation is likely to be the key to ethnic integration, not socioeconomic status. Second, they emphasize the importance of the structure of racial and ethnic inequality for understanding group distinctiveness and group preservation. And finally, they confirm the importance of a crucial variable in ethnic integration, that of the context of migration.

If we wish to speak of ethnic integration, the more pertinent questions are now: What group are we talking about and where are they located? And secondly, under what conditions do these processes occur? Further extensions of this study could go in a multitude of directions. In order to examine cross-national patterns in panethnic residential concentration levels and processes, a future study would compare the experience of similar groups in other immigrant-hosting societies, such as Australia. Another avenue for research would expand the range of groups. A third would expand the range of metropolitan areas for the same groups studied here. This would provide the most interesting analysis as it would shed further light on the link between the context of migration and ethnic distinctiveness.

The multiple lines of comparison examined here point to the connections between the national and local context, group characteristics and contexts of migration and residential integration. We have learned that the national context, race and ethnic relations in particular, operates through local structures to affect residential patterns but that these local structures do not necessarily take primacy in influencing residential integration over group-related characteristics, including the reasons for immigration, political or economic. In sum, this study underscores the ethnic character of residential incorporation and the importance of the migration context, as well as local and national conditions. The results demonstrate that the national context plays a significant role in the way ethnic boundaries influence the spatial distribution of ethnic groups in the urban neighborhoods of Canada and the United States. This study also showed the incredible insight we gain from a comparative study. We have moved beyond thinking of the integration process as being determined solely by the ability of groups and group members and only by comparing groups in different contexts can we learn something about how the structural and ideological environment, and the context of migration and reception shape group outcomes. For these reasons, there is a need to place a greater emphasis on group- and context-specific analyses in the era of the new immigration.

APPENDIX A
Fourteen ethnic groups in the U.S. and Canada

Contemporary ethnic group characteristics provide one snapshot of a historical process that is shaped by a myriad of conditions within both countries of origin and destination. It is the interplay of these bilateral conditions - such as the opportunity structure and the level of economic development and growth, geo-political conditions, age structure, past migration flows, and migration policies (Kim 2007) - which structure the composition of potential and actual migrants and hence ethnic communities. For these reasons, we should not expect to find ethnic groups mirrored with their counterparts across geo-political borders.

The extent to which ethnic communities are unique in their social and economic characteristics across national borders is explored. A comparison of community composition of the fourteen ethnic groups in the study sample, across Canada and the United States, is provided using data from the 2000 U.S. census and the 2001 Canadian census. This comparison, in terms of group size, gender, marriage, older adults, foreign-born, language, education, and income and employment, gives us an indication not only of the types of people that were attracted by each of these two countries but also those that may have been produced by them. It is important to note that these data do not permit us to determine, for some of the acquired traits, whether these qualities existed prior to immigration or subsequent to it.

GROUP PRESENCE

The chart in Figure A.1 presents ethnic group sizes for groups with less than 7 million members in the U.S. and the inset graph shows the three largest U.S. groups, English, Germans and Italians. Given that the United States has a total population that is almost tenfold the population of Canada, it is not surprising to find that all ethnic groups are larger in the U.S. compared to their counterparts in Canada. Although the rank order is less than perfect, we also observe the tendency for larger groups in the U.S. to be larger in Canada. This applies to European groups such as English, Germans and Italians. At the opposite end of the spectrum are Iranians, Haitians, and Pakistanis in both countries.

A basic calculation of the ratio of group sizes in the U.S. to Canada shows that almost all groups have a disproportionate presence in the U.S. compared to Canada. The ratio of the population of the U.S. to Canada is 9.4 and six ethnic groups fall above that figure: English, Italian, German, Polish, Korean and Russian. These groups are all disproportionately greater in the U.S.[20] Seven groups (Chinese, Asian/East Indian, Filipino, Jamaican, Iranian, Haitian, Pakistani) are disproportionately greater in size in Canada. Notably, these are most of the non-white groups. The Vietnamese ratio falls at the same level as the total population.

THE GENDER BALANCE

Figure A.2 shows the percentage of females by ethnic group in each country. For the most part, comparable ethnic groups across the border are similar in terms of their gender composition, hovering around the 50 per cent mark. More than half of the groups have more females than males in both countries. Jamaicans and Filipinos have more than 1.2 women per man in their respective communities. In contrast, Iranians and Pakistanis have a shortage of women, their ratios falling between .79 and .87. Comparing across countries, a few of the groups, Haitian, Indian, and Filipino, have slightly higher percentages of women on the Canadian side than on the U.S. side. Koreans, on the other hand, are more female in the U.S. compared to Canada.

---

[20] Using the proportion of single ancestry individuals that was estimated from the 2000 US IPUMS data (see Appendix B) for each the five groups that have a high proportion of multi-ethnic individuals, I find that only the English and Italian fell in the other direction, i.e. they were disproportionately lower in the US. The others, German, Polish and Russian, remained disproportionately greater in the US.

Figure A.1 Ethnic group sizes in Canada and the United States

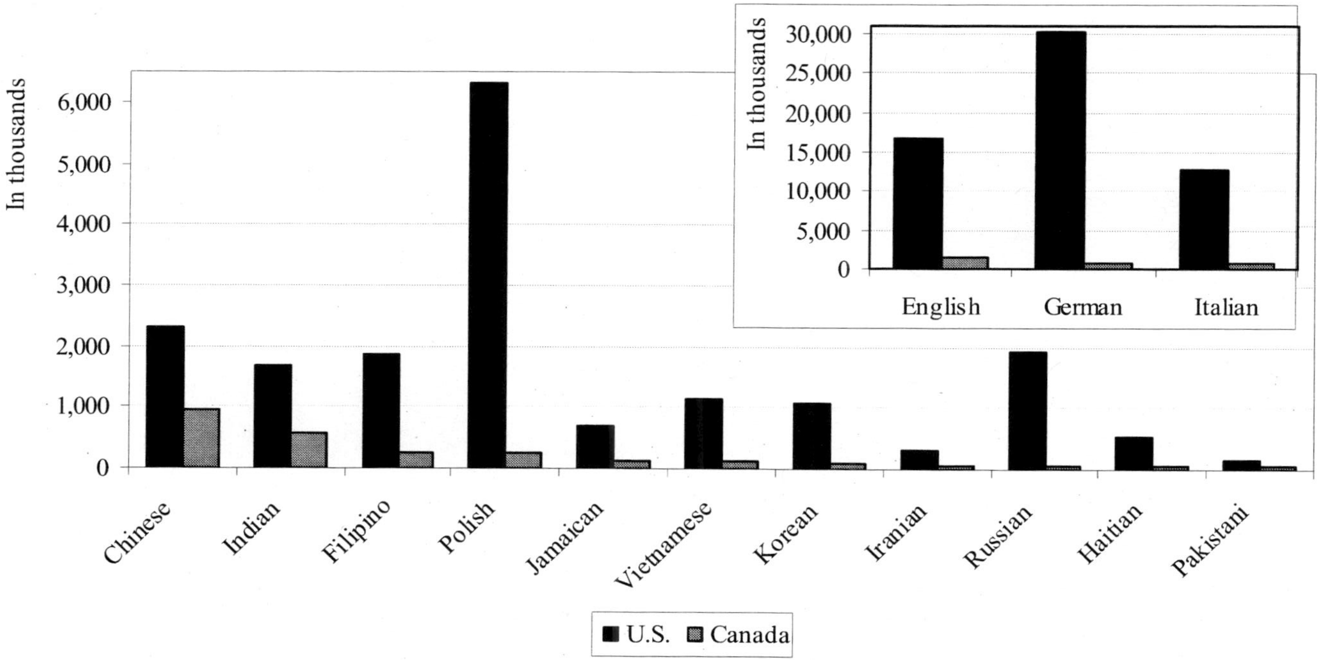

Figure A.2 Percentage of females

THE MARRIED POPULATION

In terms of the married population, ethnic groups are similar across the Canadian and U.S. border. Variation exists in the percentage married across the fourteen ethnic groups as shown in the graph. Two ethnic groups, Jamaican and Haitian, are especially conspicuous as having greater percentages of unmarried individuals in relation to the other twelve groups. They are the only two groups in the study sample to be comprised of less than 50 per cent married. Moreover, this was consistent in the U.S. and in Canada, although these two groups are even less likely to be married on the Canadian side. At the other extreme are the Indians and Pakistanis, where approximately two thirds of their communities are married on both sides of the border.

OLDER ADULTS

The five European groups are comprised of an older age structure than the Iranians, Caribbean and Asian ethnic groups (Figure A.4).[21] This is most especially pronounced among the groups in Canada, where there is a 25-point difference between the English and Pakistanis. In the U.S., this difference falls at 15-points between the same two groups. This is evidence not only of a more long-standing immigrant stream for the Europeans but may be partly attributed to the low fertility rates of the European stock in both countries.

For most of the groups, there are no differences greater than 3-points across the Canada/U.S. divide. However, for four of the groups, English, German, Italian and Polish, there is about a 7 to 12 point difference with their counterparts in the U.S. For these groups, along with Asian/East Indians, an older age structure exists in Canada than in the U.S.. The opposite pattern is evident for Iranians and Filipinos.

---

[21] The IPUMS data for the five aforementioned ethnic groups show a greater proportion of older adults in the single ancestry samples. Single ancestry Italians, Polish and Russians have a greater older population in the US than in Canada. The largest spread falls between the Polish and the Pakistanis at 21-points.

Figure A.3 Percentage of married individuals, 15 years and over

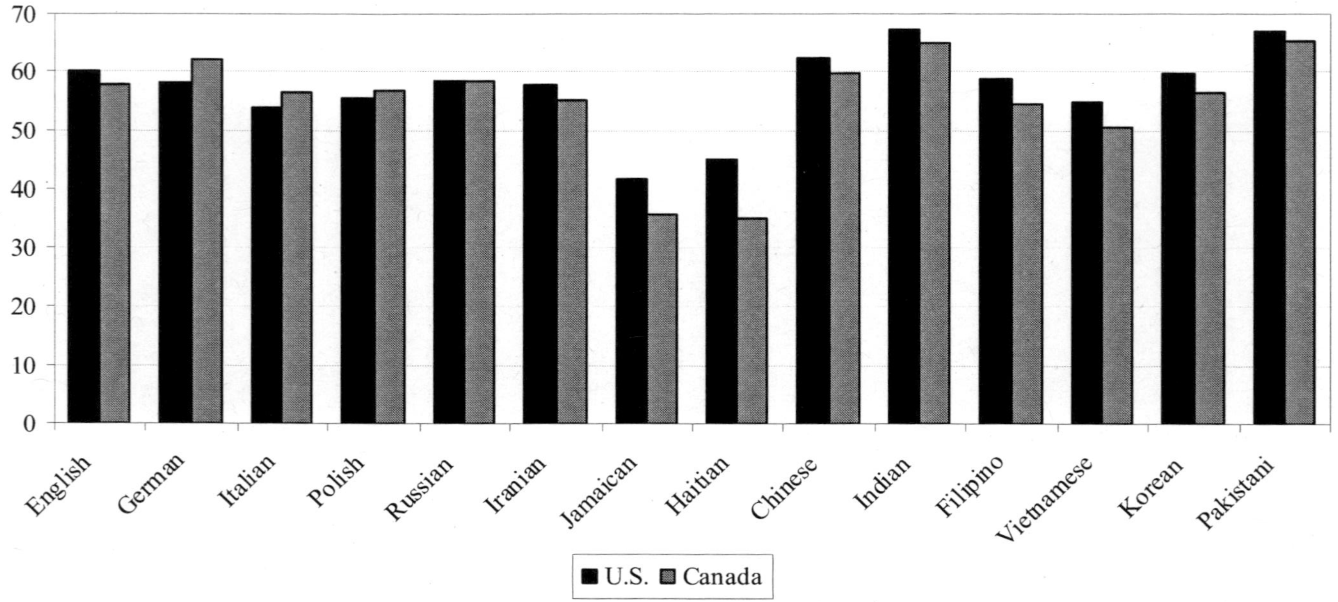

Figure A.4 Percentage of older adults, 65 years and over

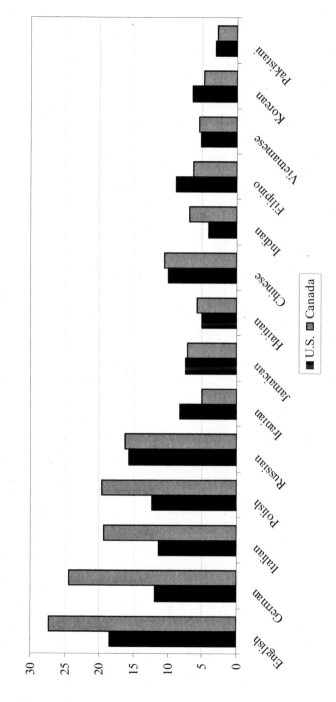

THE FOREIGN-BORN

Over 60 per cent of all nine non-European groups are foreign-born and this is consistent across the border. Iranians in Canada are clearly the most likely to be foreign-born (91 per cent), and are more so than their counterparts in the U.S. (68 per cent). Koreans and Pakistanis in Canada are also comprised of a large percentage foreign-born, 86 and 80 per cent, respectively, and are more foreign-born than their U.S. counterparts. The chart also distinctly shows that the five European groups have much larger foreign-born fractions in Canada than in the U.S.[22]

Figure A.6 presents the percentage of the foreign-born that arrived within the ten-year period prior to the census. In this dimension, there is wide variation across the ethnic groups as well as across borders. The graph shows that in both countries, large shares of the foreign-born in the Russian (68 and 79 per cent, U.S. and Canada, respectively) and Pakistani (59 and 77 per cent, U.S. and Canada, respectively) communities are recent arrivals. These two groups, as well as four others, Iranian, Chinese, Filipino, Korean, have greater proportions of newcomers among their foreign-born in Canada than in the U.S. European ethnic groups in the U.S., with the exception of Russians, have higher proportions of newcomers than comparable groups in Canada.

ABILITY TO SPEAK ENGLISH

This characteristic also resulted in wide variation across groups and countries. While there are issues with respect to the reliability of measures across contexts, thereby compromising our ability to compare across countries, they do provide some indication of the degree to which ethnic groups are linguistically excluded from mainstream society and permits some cautious cross-country comparisons. For U.S. groups, Figure A.7 provides a visual representation of those whose ability to speak English is "not well" or "not at all." On the Canadian side, the figure displays the extent to which respondents to the census indicated

---

[22] This finding is also consistent with data from IPUMS. Although the foreign-born proportions are higher in the single ancestry samples, they do not approximate the levels found in the same groups in Canada or other ethnic groups in the US.

that they could not speak English or French well enough to conduct a conversation. (Appendix B provides a discussion on the comparability of census data.)

For several groups, English language barriers are virtually non-existent in both countries (English, German, Jamaican), falling below 1 percent. Except for Italians and Polish, Russians and Asian/East Indians, groups are more linguistically excluded from the mainstream in the U.S. than in Canada.[23] This was especially pronounced among Haitians, Filipinos and Vietnamese. Russian and Asian/East Indian communities in the U.S. are similar to their respective communities in Canada.

EDUCATION

Figure A.8 graphs the percentage of each ethnic group with a Bachelor's degree or higher. It is readily observable that for all groups, but Korean, the U.S. contingent has higher levels of education.[24] This is informative in light of the characterization of the Canadian immigration policy as being more selective than the U.S. policy.

Moreover, the most highly educated groups in Canada are not the same as in the U.S. In descending order, Koreans (47 per cent), Iranians (45 per cent) and Pakistanis (43 per cent) in Canada have the largest fraction of university educated. In the U.S., the top three groups are Asian/East Indian, Iranian and Russian, with 64, 57 and 55 per cent, respectively. The groups with the lowest levels of members with university degrees are also not consistent with the exception of Jamaicans. In Canada, the English, Germans and Jamaicans have the lowest levels of educated group members compared with other ethnic groups. In the U.S., Jamaicans, Vietnamese and Haitians tend to have lower educational levels in comparison with others.

---

[23] With IPUMS data, the single ancestry proportion speaking English "not well" or "not at all" virtually doubled for Italians, Polish and Russians. While Italians in the US remained less linguistically excluded than those in Canada, this level increased for the Polish and Russians beyond that found for the same groups in Canada.

[24] Gaps between countries diminish in the single ancestry sample for the five European groups but continue to remain high for English and Germans.

Figure A.5 Percentage of foreign-born

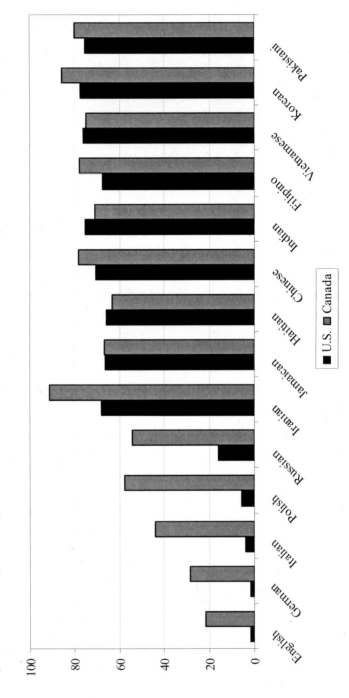

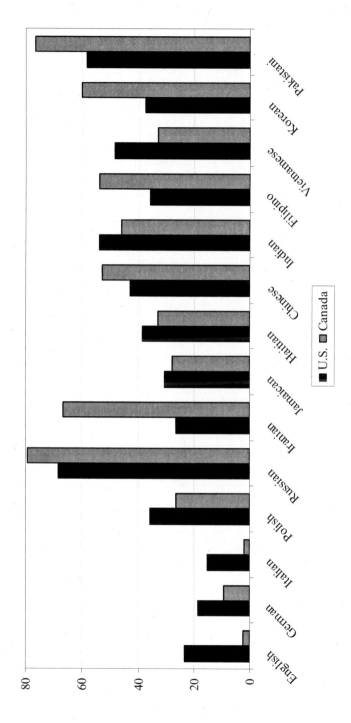

Figure A.6 Percentage of foreign-born that are newcomers

Figure A.7 Percentage with poor conversational English (and/or French in Canada)

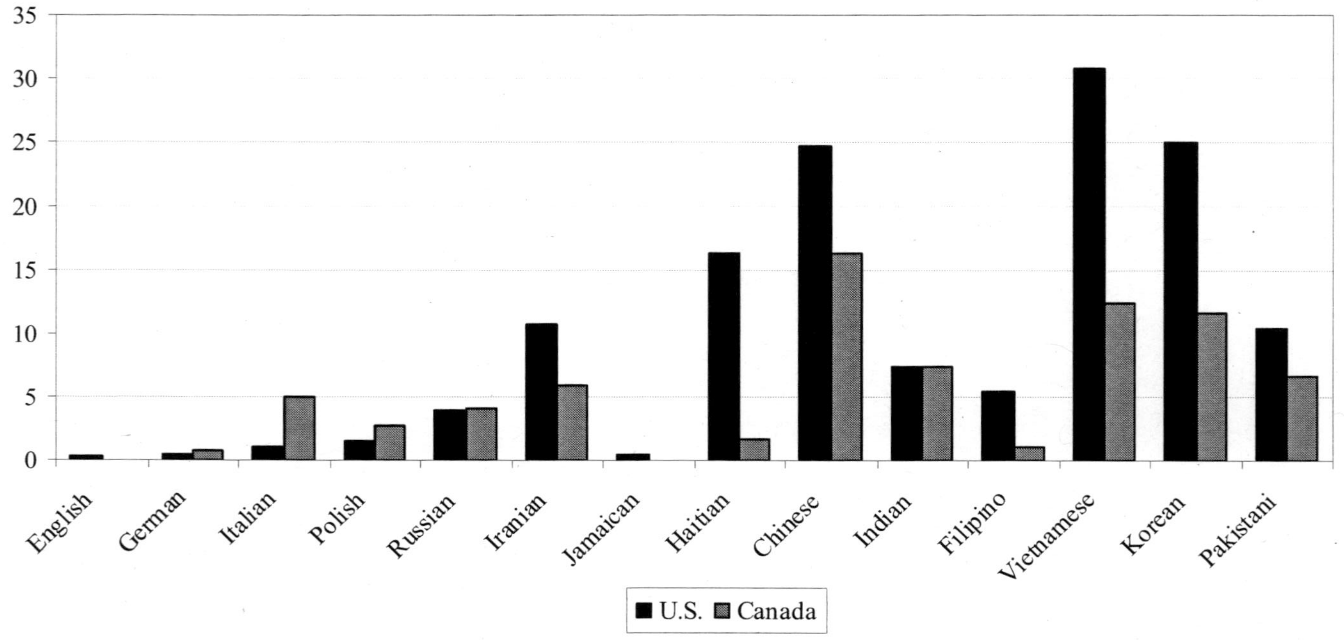

Figure A.8 Percentage with Bachelor's degree or higher, 25 years and over

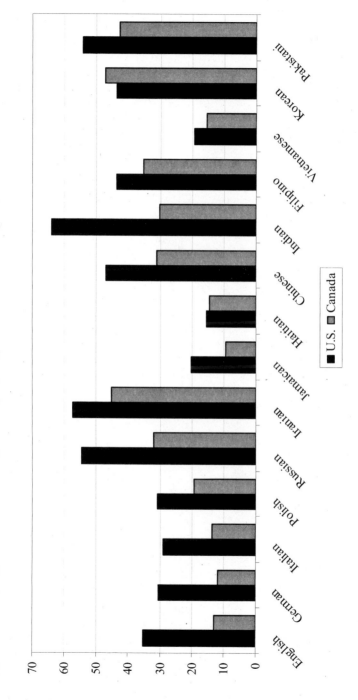

INCOME AND EMPLOYMENT

Figure A.9 presents median income for males with income, 15 years of age and older across the fourteen ethnic groups and countries (in the currency of origin). Given that the median income for U.S. males was USD$27,932 for the same period and CDN$29,276 for males in Canada, we should expect slightly higher values for groups in Canada. However, we see that male members of ethnic groups in Canada are not doing as well as their counterparts in the U.S. with respect to income. The Vietnamese may be the only exception as the Canadian contingent earned slightly more income in Canadian dollars than did their U.S. contingent in U.S. dollars.

Unemployment figures show the higher levels of unemployment for the Canadian contingent of all fourteen ethnic groups. We also observe that some groups are faring worse than others. Haitians and Jamaicans have the highest unemployment rates of all groups in the U.S. Haitians also top Canada's list of highest unemployment rates followed closely by Pakistanis and Iranians. These groups faced unemployment rates above 10 per cent.

Self-employment rates remain fairly consistent for the comparable ethnic groups across the border, with a few exceptions. Where differences are found, groups in Canada tend to have higher levels of self-employment. This can be observed for the English, Germans, Italians, Polish, Chinese and Koreans.

Comparing across groups, Jamaicans, Haitians and Filipinos tend to have the lowest self-employment rates in both countries falling at a rate of 4 per cent. Germans in Canada, and Iranians and Koreans in both countries, are the most likely to be self-employed. For the most part, self-employment rates are below 20 per cent. But for Germans and Koreans in Canada, this reaches beyond 20 per cent, going as high as 32 percent for the latter group.

Figure A.9 Median income of males with income, 15 years and over

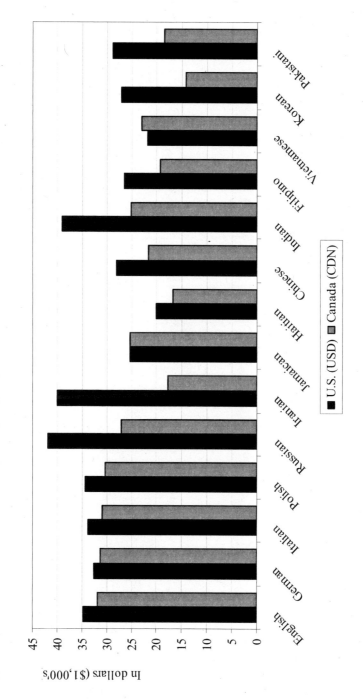

In dollars ($ 1,000's)

■ U.S. (USD) ▨ Canada (CDN)

Figure A.10 Percentage unemployed

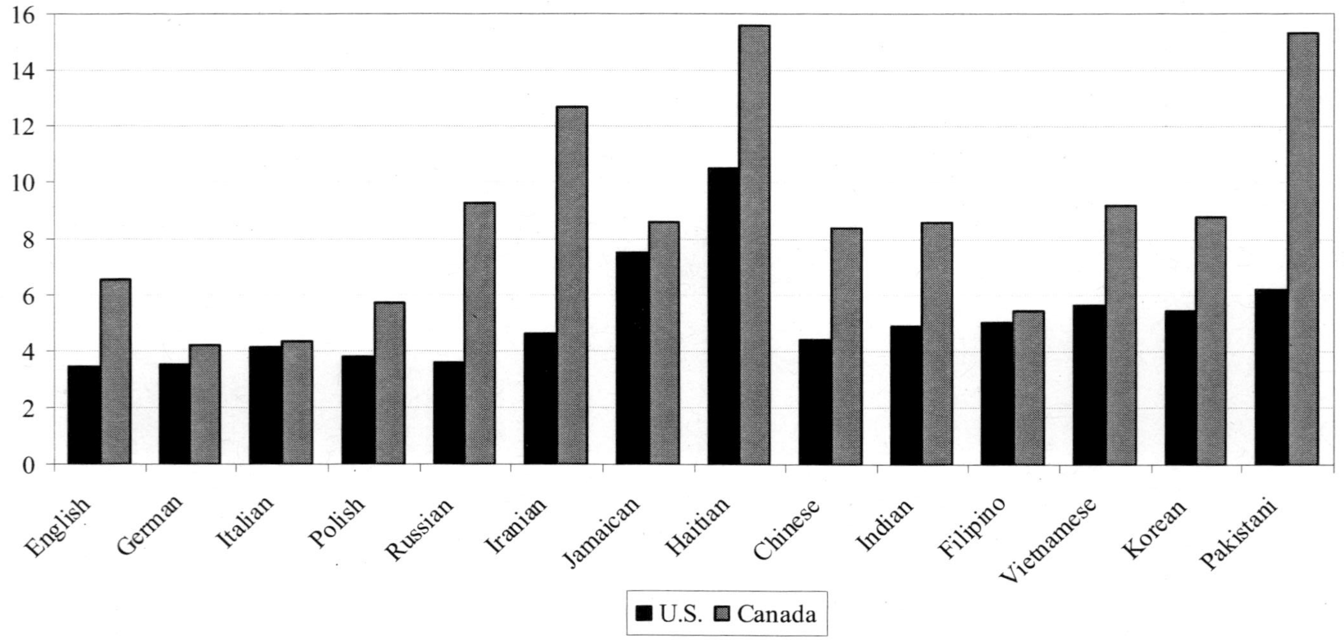

Figure A.11 Percentage self-employed

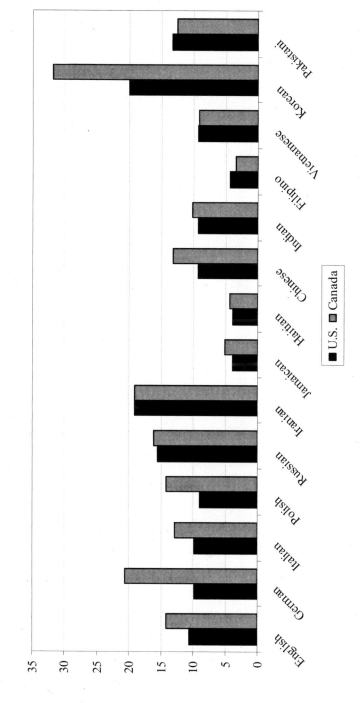

Table A.1 Religious affiliation for ethnic groups in Canada

Ethnic group	Dominant religion(s), percentage
English	Protestant, 63
German	Protestant, 57
Italian	Catholic, 92
Polish	Catholic, 83
Russian	Christian Orthodox, 28; No religion, 27
Iranian	Muslim, 74
Jamaican	Protestant, 57
Haitian	Catholic, 58
Chinese	No religion, 60
Indian	Sikh, 37; Hindu, 30
Filipino	Catholic, 83
Vietnamese	Buddhist, 48; Catholic, 24
Korean	Protestant, 32; Catholic, 24
Pakistani	Muslim, 93

RELIGION

Religious affiliation is measured in the Census of Canada but is not available in the U.S. census. Although we cannot compare religious compositions across countries, they may be similar and I present the Canadian results here. Table A.1 presents religious affiliation for the majority of ethnic group members. As identified in the list, religion crosscuts ethnicity to some extent. That is, Protestant and Catholic are the two most common religions, covering over half the populations of seven ethnic groups. And for several of these groups and others, there is a high degree of religious homogeneity within ethnic boundaries. For instance, Italians, Filipinos and the Polish are comprised of more than 80 per cent Catholic, and Iranians and Pakistanis are highly Muslim groups. Russians, Asian/East Indians, Vietnamese and Koreans are characterized by religious heterogeneity.

SUMMARY

This profile of ethnic groups across countries along various dimensions suggests that communities are similar in some respects but diverge in others. In general, ethnic communities are similar across countries in their gender composition and in their married population, although the two Caribbean groups are less likely to be married in Canada. Important systematic differences also emerge. U.S. ethnic groups are doing better economically than comparable groups in Canada. Those in the U.S. are more likely to have university degrees (with the exception of Koreans), higher median incomes for males (exceptions: Jamaicans and Vietnamese), and lower unemployment rates.

This suggests that we must be cautious in assuming that groups in the U.S. are similar to their counterparts in Canada as there are some significant differences. These differences are indicative of two processes; the first is that the two countries attract different types of migrants to some degree, and the second is that the two countries offer different opportunities to their respective ethnic groups. These social and economic factors must be taken into account when comparing ethnic group outcomes across countries.

APPENDIX B

A comparison of census data

The census has a long tradition in Canada and in the United States. The first national census in the U.S. began in 1790 and did not appear in Canada until 81 years later, in 1871. For both countries, the census was developed to determine appropriate representation in government by providing a count of the population. As a state responsibility then, a government agency has been mandated to collect and disseminate the census in each country, the Bureau of the Census in the U.S. Department of Commerce, and Statistics Canada.

The census is conducted decennially in the U.S. and quinquennially in Canada and measures population and housing characteristics in each country. These data have long been used beyond the purpose for which they originated. Numerous studies by independent researchers have been made possible by public access to the data. However, despite all these shared characteristics, differences in measurement exist between the two censuses, which are important considerations for comparative studies. In this appendix, I show how two recent censuses (1 April 2000 in the U.S. and 15 May 2001 in Canada) compare with respect to the variables of interest. The first part deals with geographic concepts and then I address population and housing variables.

MEASURES OF GEOGRAPHIC CONCEPTS

Both countries define several layers of geographic areas to aid in the collection and dissemination of data. These spatial areas then become the basis for population and housing analyses. In the present study, three geographic boundaries are of interest. The first is the geo-political border

185

that demarcates nation-states. The second and third are metropolitan areas and census tracts, respectively. The latter two are addressed in turn.

The US Census defines Metropolitan Statistical Areas or Consolidated Metropolitan Statistical Areas (MSA/CMSA) in the following terms:

> . A core area with a large population nucleus, plus adjacent communities having a high degree of economic and social integration with that core. Qualification of an MSA requires the presence of a city with 50,000 or more inhabitants and a total population of at least 100,000 (75,000 in New England). An area becomes a CMSA if it meets the requirements to qualify as a metropolitan statistical area, has a population of 1,000,000 or more.

The Canadian equivalent is the Census Metropolitan Area:

> An area consisting of one or more adjacent municipalities situated around a major urban core. To form a census metropolitan area, the urban core must have a population of at least 100,000.

These geographic areas are comparable in size between the two countries although U.S. metropolitan areas tend to be larger with a mean metropolitan population of 819,000 as opposed to 707,000 in Canada. The range is also much greater in the U.S., from 58,000 to 21 million. In Canada, the range falls between 120,000 and 4.6 million.

A smaller level of geography relevant for this study is the census tract, which is also measured in both countries. The U.S. definition states:

> Designed to be relatively homogeneous units with respect to population characteristics, economic status, and living conditions at the time of establishment, census tracts average about 4,000 inhabitants.

And in Canada:

> An area that is small and relatively stable. Census tracts

usually have a population of 2,500 to 8,000.

Past studies have also used these levels for comparative analysis (White, Fong and Cai 2003).

POPULATION VARIABLES

Ethnic ancestry

Ethnic ancestry was asked of a 20 per cent sample of households in each country. While the definition of ethnic ancestry is similar across the two most recent censuses (Table B.1) and both allow for multiple responses (up to 2 coded in the U.S., 4 in Canada), the tabulations provided by the census offices differ.

The U.S. Census collects ancestry information for all respondents but disseminates ethnic detail only for those groups that are not captured in the Race question, namely for Blacks and Whites, and all others that have been categorized as "other." Asian ethnic groups, American Indians and Alaska Natives, Native Hawaiian and other Pacific Islanders are not captured under ancestry. Responses available from this question are provided in a series of four tables, PCT15 to PCT18, in Summary File 3. The first table, PCT15, provides a count of the population giving single and multiple responses but does not specify the ethnic origin. The next three tables, PCT16 to PCT18, present a list of ethnic identities given first by respondents, and then second ancestries, and finally, a total count of responses, respectively. For Asian groups, PCT5 in SF1, provide data on single origin Asian subgroups. Statistics Canada also collects ancestry information for all respondents and it also disseminates a list consisting of 100 ethnic groups by single, multiple and total responses. Their tabulation preserves ethnic detail by single and multiple ancestries.

Table B.1 Census details on ethnic origins

U.S.

Census question

What is this person's ancestry or ethnic origin? (For example: Italian, Jamaican, African Am., Cambodian, Cape Verdean, Norwegian, Dominican, French Canadian, Haitian, Korean, Lebanese, Polish, Nigerian, Mexican, Taiwanese, Ukrainian, and so on.)

Census definition

Ancestry refers to a person's ethnic origin or descent, "roots," heritage, or the place of birth of the person, the person's parents, or their ancestors before their arrival in the United States.

Canada

Census question

While most people in Canada view themselves as Canadians, information on their ancestral origins has been collected since the 1901 Census to capture the changing composition of Canada's diverse population. Therefore, this question refers to the origins of the person's ancestors. To which ethnic or cultural group(s) did this person's ancestors belong? For example, Canadian, French, English, Chinese, Italian, German, Scottish, Irish, Cree, Micmac, Métis, Inuit (Eskimo), East Indian, Ukrainian, Dutch, Polish, Portuguese, Filipino, Jewish, Greek, Jamaican, Vietnamese, Lebanese, Chilean, Somali, etc.

Census definition

An ancestor is someone from whom a person is descended and is usually more distant than a grandparent. Other than Aboriginal persons, most people can trace their origins to their ancestors who first came to this continent. Ancestry should not be confused with citizenship or nationality.

The analysis concentrates on individuals with single ethnic origins and ethnic tabulations are likely to be comparable across borders, more so for the Asian subgroups - Chinese, Filipino, Asian/East Indian, Korean, Pakistani and Vietnamese - and less so for the White and Black ethnic subgroups. The single response tabulation for Asian groups in Canada may be akin to the "Asian alone" tabulation under race in the U.S. For the other U.S. groups in the sample, the numbers represent all first ancestry responses and include individuals with multiple ancestries.

This feature would have a bearing upon the comparability of groups to the extent that an ethnic group is comprised of a large proportion of multiple ancestry individuals. Data from the *Integrated Public Use Microdata Series* (IPUMS-1 percent sample), an individual-level dataset drawn from the 2000 census provide some clues on this matter. The eight non-Asian groups were selected using the First Ancestry variable from the IPUMS sample, English, German, Italian, Polish, Russian, Iranian, Jamaican and Haitian, and then assessed to what extent their populations consisted of individuals with a single ancestry. The results are shown in Table B.2.

Five out of the eight ethnic groups have substantial proportions of individuals with multiple ancestries, where more than one third identify with a second ethnic origin. Less than 8 percent of each of the three remaining groups, those that listed Iranian, Jamaican and Haitian as their first ancestry, were found to have a second ethnic origin. For these groups, at least, comparability with Canadian data may be maintained. For the others, segregation values may be dampened to the extent that multiple ancestry is associated with residential integration. English, Germans, Italians, Polish and Russians would be the most affected.

Both the U.S. and Canadian censuses asked questions regarding nativity and year of arrival. Whereas the nativity question was worded in exactly the same manner across the two (i.e. *Where was this person born?*), the year of arrival question differs. Differences were found in the tabulations that were disseminated, as responses to questions on nativity, citizenship and year of arrival were used for organizing data.

Table B.2 Percent of group with single ancestry of all first ancestries

Ethnic group	Percent	Two most common 2nd ancestries
English	50.6	German (13.6), Irish (13.3)
German	49.7	Irish (14.7), English (8.8)
Italian	58.7	Irish (11.5), German (9.3)
Polish	58.4	German (11.7), Irish (6.9)
Russian	65.4	Polish (10.5), German (5.9)
Iranian	94.3	German (1.1), Armenian (0.7)
Jamaican	92.9	African-American (1.6), African (0.5)
Haitian	96.7	African-American (0.), Jamaican (0.5)

With respect to nativity, the U.S. used the classification of native-born and foreign-born, where the foreign-born included all those who were not U.S. citizens at birth, such as immigrants (i.e. legal permanent residents), temporary migrants, humanitarian migrants and unauthorized migrants. Canadian data, on the other hand, distinguished by immigrant status and used three categories: 1. Non-immigrant population (Canadian citizens by birth); 2. Immigrant population (i.e. landed immigrants); and 3. Non-permanent resident population (i.e. employment authorized migrants, students, those with Minister's permits, refugee claimants and family members). These counts were made comparable by combining the immigrant population and non-permanent resident population in the Canadian data.

Education

The U.S. Census contained one question on educational attainment; *What is the highest degree of level of school this person has completed?* The Canadian Census asked a series of questions for only those aged 15 and over regarding their highest level of elementary or secondary school attended, years completed at university and/or another post-secondary institution, and certificates, diplomas or degrees obtained.

One aggregation of educational attainment in the U.S. Census restricted the population to those aged 25 years and above. To maintain comparability, a special tabulation of the highest educational attainment for same population in Canada was requested. The proportion of those with Bachelor's degrees or higher can then be determined and compared across countries.

Income and labor force characteristics

Questions about income and labor force participation were asked of the population 15 years and older in both countries. Median income across the countries is highly comparable as it is based on individuals 15 years and over with income.

The grouping of the labor force into industries is based on an identical classification scheme, the 1997 North American Industry Classification System (NAICS), created to enhance industry comparability across the three North American Free Trade Agreement (NAFTA) trading partners (Canada, United States and Mexico). Thus, the industry variable is directly comparable across borders.

To determine membership in the labor force, a series of questions was asked in both censuses regarding employment information and work activity. In the U.S., the civilian labor force (employed and unemployed) was distinguished from those in the armed forces. Those not in the labor force included students, individuals taking care of home or family, retired workers, off-season seasonal workers not looking for work, institutionalized population, and those doing incidental unpaid family work. The Canadian census did not make the distinction between military and civilian in the labor force (employed and unemployed) but grouped them together.

With respect to self-employment, both countries asked respondents to identify their occupation and whether they were self-employed in an incorporated or non-incorporated business, professional practice or farm. This variable could be considered to be highly comparable across datasets.

Religion

Religious affiliation was not collected in the U.S. Census but was available in Canada, where individuals were asked to indicate a denomination even if he/she is not a practicing member. Ninety categories are listed in the full table.

Housing

In the U.S., an occupied housing unit included the usual place of residence of a person or group. This included rooms in hotels and boarding houses. All occupied housing units were classified as owner-occupied or renter-occupied. The Canadian data also defined a dwelling as the usual place of residence of a person of a group of persons but made a distinction between private and collective dwellings, or rooming houses, hotels, hospitals, etc. This distinction makes the U.S. classification scheme more encompassing than the Canadian one, which means that there were likely to be lower owner-occupied rates in the U.S. than in Canada. In other words, owner-occupied rates would be higher in the U.S. if we applied the Canadian definition since the denominator would likely decrease. Finally, the terms, *Period of Construction* in Canada and *Year Structure Built* in the U.S., refer to the same concept; that of the construction of the building, and not when it was remodeled, added to, or converted.

The question of selection bias

The restricted numbers of census tracts that were included in the analysis in Chapters Six and Seven raise the question of selection bias since tracts with smaller numbers of group members were systematically excluded. The consequence of omitting these tracts from the analysis is that the degree of residential concentration may be biased upward for each of the four groups in both places. In other words, higher levels of concentration were found than we would have otherwise estimated if all tracts that contained at least one ethnic group member were included. This might have also led to problems in the results of the regression analysis, most likely in dampening the effect of acculturation and socioeconomic resources. This would be the case if ethnic group members that are the most residentially integrated are also highly acculturated and have higher socioeconomic status.

Fortunately, the Canadian census tabulations included all tracts with at least 10 ethnic group members. (These data were limited in the main analysis to maintain comparability with U.S. data.) Using the more complete Canadian census data, I assess the degree of possible selection bias by re-analyzing the Canadian data for all four ethnic groups, Chinese, Jamaicans, Iranians and Vietnamese, in two metropolitan areas each. The summary statistics in Tables C.1 and C.2 show, by ethnic group and metropolitan area, the selected ethnic group characteristics of the mean tract in this data pool.

Table C.1 Summary statistics, Chinese and Jamaicans

Group	Variables	Toronto	Vancouver	Montréal
Chinese	Number of tracts	865	374	n/a
	Mean tract size (logged)	8.47 (.4)	8.47 (.4)	n/a
	Mean group proportion	.08 (.1)	.16 (.2)	n/a
	Proportion foreign-born	.74 (.2)	.75 (.1)	n/a
	Proportion university degree	.36 (.2)	.31 (.2)	n/a
	Proportion self-employed	.08 (.1)	.10 (.1)	n/a
Jamaicans	Number of tracts	822	n/a	196
	Mean tract size (logged)	8.50 (.4)	n/a	8.33 (.4)
	Mean group proportion	.03 (.03)	n/a	.01 (.01)
	Proportion foreign-born	.56 (.2)	n/a	.51 (.3)
	Proportion university degree	.15 (.2)	n/a	.17 (.3)
	Proportion self-employed	.06 (.1)	n/a	.05 (.2)

Note: Standard deviation in parenthesis.

Table C.2 Summary statistics, Iranians and Vietnamese

Group	Variables	Toronto	Vancouver	Montréal
Iranians	Number of tracts	519	213	n/a
	Mean tract size (logged)	8.51 (.4)	8.58 (.3)	n/a
	Mean group proportion	.02 (.02)	.02 (.02)	n/a
	Proportion foreign-born	.80 (.2)	.82 (.2)	n/a
	Proportion university degree	.40 (.4)	.37 (.3)	n/a
	Proportion self-employed	.12 (.2)	.12 (.2)	n/a
Vietnamese	Number of tracts	434	n/a	367
	Mean tract size (logged)	8.55 (.4)	n/a	8.22 (.4)
	Mean group proportion	.01 (.02)	n/a	.02 (.02)
	Proportion foreign-born	.78 (.2)	n/a	.76 (.2)
	Proportion university degree	.14 (.3)	n/a	.34 (.4)
	Proportion self-employed	.06 (.2)	n/a	.09 (.2)

Note: Standard deviation in parenthesis.

We can compare this table with Tables 6.6 and 6.7 in Chapter Six for the relevant group and metropolitan area. For the Chinese in Toronto, we find that the mean tract size is smaller than the more restricted dataset. Not surprisingly, the mean group proportion is also lower, to half the proportion of the main sample. The more inclusive sample is also slightly less foreign-born and slightly more university educated suggesting that the Chinese population in more integrated neighborhoods is also more likely to be native-born and highly educated. There is no difference in the proportion self-employed. Similar results are obtained for the Chinese in Vancouver. The differences in the selected characteristics of tracts in the two samples are not large.

The mean proportions of foreign-born or self-employed Jamaicans in Toronto tracts (where there are at least 10 members) are similar to the mean proportions in the more restricted sample (Table C.1). However, in terms of education, the more inclusive sample finds higher levels of university degree holders. This suggests that there may be a stronger association than we observed between education and residential concentration for Jamaicans in this Canadian metro. Montréal was excluded from the main analysis but I include it here for comparison.

Summary statistics for Iranians in Toronto and Vancouver are provided in Table C.2. A comparison of these descriptives with the descriptives presented in Chapter Six, Table 6.7 reveals that the inclusion of tracts with fewer Iranians brings down the proportion foreign-born and university educated. Self-employment remains similar, although slightly lower proportions can be observed for the more inclusive Vancouver sample of tracts. For Iranians then, the main analysis is likely to show a stronger association between residential concentration and acculturation or socioeconomic resources than is actually the case.

Finally, the more inclusive sample of tracts with the Vietnamese in Toronto in Table C.2 (Montréal is also included here) reveals higher levels of foreign-born, university degrees and self-employment. In light of these descriptives, it is likely that the effect of education is stronger than observed in the main analysis. The opposite is likely for the effect of acculturation (i.e. proportion foreign-born).

Tables C.3 and C.4 report the results from the multivariate interaction analysis on the logit of proportion co-ethnic for the four groups; Chinese and Iranians in Toronto and Vancouver (Table C.3) and Jamaicans and Vietnamese in Toronto and Montréal (Table C.4). Graphs depicting the associations found in the regression models are presented in Figures C.1 and C.2, holding covariates constant and converting back to the original scale.[25]

Table C.3 Chinese and Iranians in Toronto and Vancouver

	Chinese	Iranians
Proportion univ. degree	-.151	.247 **
Degree*Vancouver	-.566	.211
Proportion foreign-born	1.827 **	.572 **
Foreign*Vancouver	1.114 **	.104
Proportion self-employed	-.280	.311
Self*Vancouver	-1.873 **	-.209
Metropolitan area (TO omitted)	--	--
Vancouver	.350	-.003
Tract size (logged)	-.029	-.461 **
Constant	-4.219 **	-1.375
Adjust R^2	.12 **	.06 **
N	1,239	732

*p<.1; ** p<.05

[25] Values for covariates are as follows: proportion university degree .3, proportion foreign-born .3, proportion self-employed .1, and tract size 5,000.

Figure C.1 Net effect of proportion university degree on proportion co-ethnic in census tracts, Chinese and Iranians

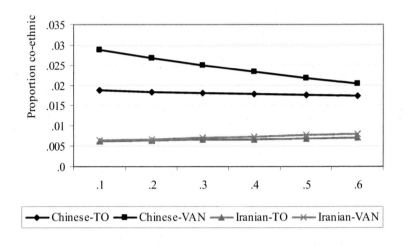

Figure C.2 Net effect of proportion foreign-born on proportion co-ethnic in census tracts, Chinese and Iranians

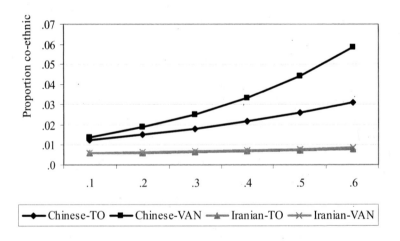

Figure C.3 Net effect of proportion self-employed on proportion co-ethnic in census tracts, Chinese and Iranians

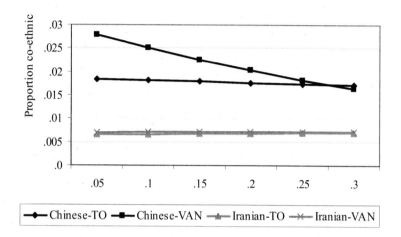

Comparing these results with those presented in Chapter Seven, Figures 7.1 to 7.3, I find that, in general, patterns for the Chinese in the two Canadian metros are relatively similar to the patterns found in the more restricted sample (Figures C.1 to C.3). The main difference lies in the level of concentration at which the Chinese start off in Vancouver (no large gap is found in Toronto). As expected, concentration levels are lower using this more inclusive sample.

Table C.4 Jamaicans and Vietnamese in Toronto and Montréal

	Jamaicans	Vietnamese
Proportion univ. degree	-1.082 **	-.315 *
Degree*Montréal	.711 **	.024
Proportion foreign-born	.295 *	-.719 **
Degree*Montréal	-.272	.668 **
Proportion self-employed	-.986 **	-.383
Degree*Montréal	.826 *	.418
Metropolitan area (TO omitted)		
Degree*Montréal	-1.085 **	.586 **
Tract size (logged)	-.037	-.610 **
Constant	-3.400 **	1.128
Adjust R^2	.21 **	.08 **
N	1,018	801

*p<.1; ** p<.05

Figure C.4 Net effect of proportion university degree on proportion co-ethnic in census tracts, Jamaicans and Vietnamese

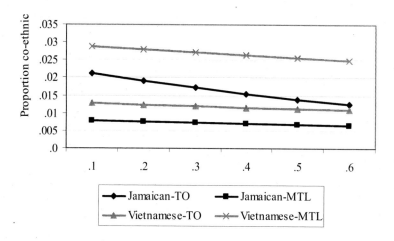

Figure C.5 Net effect of proportion foreign-born on proportion co-ethnic in census tracts, Jamaicans and Vietnamese

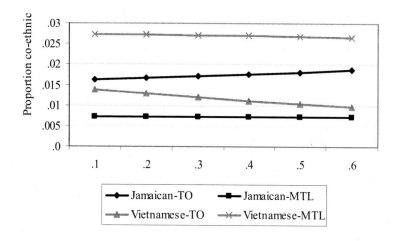

Figure C.6 Net effect of proportion university degree in census tracts for Jamaicans and Vietnamese

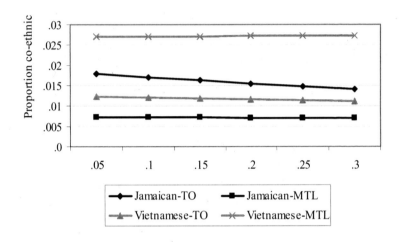

Levels for Iranians in the same two metropolitan areas are also lower in the more inclusive sample as shown in Figures C.1 to C.3. In addition, we observe differences in the associations for education and self-employment. There is a significant positive effect of education on residential concentration in contrast with the negative effect found with the limited sample (Chapter Seven, Figures 7.7 to 7.9). This is consistent for both metropolitan areas. Self-employment does not appear to have a significant effect on the residential concentration of Iranians in Toronto or Vancouver using the more inclusive sample but has a positive effect on Iranians in Vancouver using the restricted sample. In terms of the foreign-born, I find that both samples reveal a positive effect.

For Jamaicans, the effect of education and foreign-born on the proportion co-ethnic are relatively similar (Table C.4, Figures C.4 to C.6). Differences, however, could be observed for the effect of self-employment. Again, levels of concentration are lower in the more inclusive sample than in the restricted one (Chapter Seven, Figures 7.4 to 7.6).

As with the other three groups, levels of concentration are lower for the Vietnamese and the effect of education and self-employment is not noticeably different (Table C.4, Figures C.4 to C.6) from the main analysis presented in Chapter Seven. However, differences can be distinguished in terms of the proportion foreign-born, for which there is a negative association in the inclusive sample but a positive one in the restricted sample (Chapter Seven, Figures 7.10 to 7.12).

Comparing these results to those of Chapter Seven suggest that some degree of selection bias is observed but not to the extent that might be expected. That is, in general, patterns remain the same for both samples with respect to the effect of education and foreign-birth (with some exceptions). The effect of education does not change, except for Iranians, and the effect of foreign-born does not change, except for Vietnamese. The juxtaposition of results from the two samples reveal that the effect of self-employment is likely to be the most biased when omitting neighborhoods with small numbers of ethnic group members. Based on these results, it is likely that the degree of selection bias in the U.S. samples are also minimal as well, although there are likely to be exceptions. Thus, caution should be applied when generalizing findings to all neighborhoods.

References

Adams, Michael Henry. 2003. *Fire and ice: The United States, Canada and the myth of converging values*. Toronto: Penguin Canada.

Adelman, Howard. 1982. *Canada and the Indochinese refugees*. Regina: L.A. Weigl Educational Associates Ltd.

Adelman, Robert M. 2005. "The roles of race, class and residential preferences in the neighborhood racial composition of middle-class blacks and whites." *Social Science Quarterly* 86:209-228.

Alba, Richard D., and John R. Logan. 1993. "Minority proximity to whites in suburbs: An individual-level analysis of segregation." *American Journal of Sociology* 98:1388-1427.

Alba, Richard D., and Victor Nee. 1997. "Rethinking assimilation theory for a new era of immigration." *International Migration Review* 31:826-874.

Alba, Richard, John R. Logan, and Kyle Crowder. 1997. "White ethnic neighborhoods and assimilation: The greater New York region, 1980-1990." *Social Forces* 75:883-912.

Aldrich, Howard E., and Roger Waldinger. 1990. "Ethnicity and entrepreneurship." *Annual Review of Sociology* 16:111-135.

Andersen, Robert, and Tina Fetner. 2008. "Cohort differences in tolerance of homosexuality." *Public Opinion Quarterly* 72:311-330.

Arbaci, Sonia. 2008. "(Re)Viewing ethnic residential segregation in Southern European cities: Housing and urban regimes as mechanisms of marginalisation." *Housing Studies* 23:589-613.

Balakrishnan, T.R. 2001. "Residential segregation and socio-economic integration of Asians in Canadian cities." *Canadian Ethnic Studies* 33:120-132.

Balakrishnan, T.R., and Feng Hou. 1999. "Socioeconomic integration and spatial residential patterns of immigrant groups in Canada." *Population Research and Policy Review* 18:201-217.

Bashi, Vilna. 2004. "Globalized anti-blackness: Transnationalizing Western immigration law, policy and practice." *Ethnic and Racial Studies* 27:584-606.

Bashi, Vilna, and Antonio McDaniel. 1997. "A theory of immigration and racial stratification." *Journal of Black Studies* 27:668-682.

Bloemraad, Irene. 2003. "Institutions, ethnic leaders, and the political incorporation of immigrants: A comparison of Canada and the United States." Pp. 361-401 in *Host societies and the reception of immigrants*, edited by Jeffrey G. Reitz. La Jolla, CA: Center for Comparative Immigration Studies.

—. 2006. *Becoming a citizen: Incorporating immigrants and refugees in the*

United States and Canada. Berkeley, CA: University of California Press.

Borjas, George J. 1999. *Heaven's door: Immigration policy and the American economy*. Princeton, NJ: Princeton University Press.

Bouma-Doff, Wenda van der Laan. 2007. "Involuntary isolation: Ethnic preferences and residential segregation." *Journal of Urban Affairs* 29:289-309.

Boyd, Monica. 1976. "Immigration policies and trends: A comparison of Canada and the United States." *Demography* 13:83-104.

Bozorgmehr, Mehdi. 1997. "Internal ethnicity: Iranians in Los Angeles." *Sociological Perspectives* 40:387-408.

Bozorgmehr, Mehdi, and Georges Sabagh. 1988. "High status immigrants: A statistical profile of Iranians in the United States." *Iranian Studies* 21:5-36.

Breton, Raymond. 1964. "Institutional completeness of ethnic communities and the personal relations of immigrants." *American Journal of Sociology* 70:193-205.

Breton, Raymond, Wsevolod W. Isajiw, Warren E. Kalbach, and Jeffrey G. Reitz (Eds.). 1990. *Ethnic identity and equality: Varieties of experience in a Canadian city*. Toronto: University of Toronto Press.

Burnley, Ian. 1999. "Levels of immigrant residential concentration in Sydney and their relationship with disadvantage." *Urban Studies* 36:1295-1315.

Charles, Camille Zubrinsky. 2003. "The dynamics of racial residential segregation." *Annual Review of Sociology* 29:167-207.

Chavez, Leo R. 2001. *Covering immigration: Popular images and the politics of the nation*. Berkeley: University of California Press.

Chiswick, Barry R. 1982. "Immigrants in the U.S. labor market." *Annals of the American Academy of Political and Social Science* 460:64-72.

Cho, Wendy K. Tam, James G. Gimpel, and Joshua Dyck. 2006. "Residential concentration, political socialization, and voter turnout." *The Journal of Politics* 68:156-167.

Con, Harry, Ronald J. Con, Graham Johnson, Edgar Wickberg, and William E. Willmott. 1982. *From China to Canada: A history of the Chinese communities in Canada*. Toronto: McClelland and Steward Ltd.

Crowder, Kyle, and Lucky M. Tedrow. 2001. "West Indians and the residential landscape of New York." in *Islands in the city: West Indian migration to New York*, edited by Nancy Foner. Ewing, NJ: University of California Press.

Darden, Joe T. 1995. "Black residential segregation since the 1948 *Shelley v. Kraemer* decision." *Journal of Black Studies* 25:680-691.

Darden, Joe T., and Sameh M. Kamel. 2000. "Black residential segregation in suburban Detroit: Empirical testing of the ecological theory." *Review of Black Political Economy* 27:103-123.

Dawkins, Casey J. 2005. "Evidence on the intergenerational persistence of residential segregation by race." *Urban Studies* 42:545-555.

Dinardo, John, and Thomas Lemieux. 1997. "Diverging male wage inequality in the United States and Canada, 1981-1988: Do institutions explain the difference?" *Industrial and Labor Relations Review* 50:629-651.

Do, Hien Duc. 1999. *The Vietnamese Americans.* Westport, CT: Greenwood Press.

Dorais, Louis-Jacques. 1991. "Refugee adaptation and community structure: The Indochinese in Quebec City, Canada." *International Migration Review* 25:551-573.

Ellen, Ingrid Gould, Tod Mijanovich, and Keri-Nicole Dillman. 2001. "Neighborhood effects on health: Exploring the links and assessing the evidence." *Journal of Urban Affairs* 23:391-408.

Espiritu, Yen Le. 1992. *Asian American panethnicity: Bridging institutions and identities.* Philadelphia: Temple University Press.

Farley, Reynolds, and William H. Frey. 1994. "Changes in the segregation of whites from blacks during the 1980s: Small steps toward a more integrated society." *American Sociological Review* 59:23-45.

Flippen, Chenoa A. 2001. "Residential segregation and minority home ownership." *Social Science Research* 30:337-362.

Foner, Nancy. 1985. "Race and color: Jamaican migrants in London and New York City." *International Migration Review* 19:708-727.

—. 1998. "West Indian identity in the diaspora: Comparative and historical perspectives." *Latin American Perspectives* 25:173-188.

Fong, Eric. 1994. "Residential proximity among racial groups in U.S. and Canadian neighborhoods." *Urban Affairs Quarterly* 30:285-297.

—. 1996. "A comparative perspective on racial residential segregation: American and Canadian experiences." *Sociological Quarterly* 37:199-27.

Fong, Eric, and Milena Gulia. 1999. "Differences in neighborhood qualities among racial and ethnic groups in Canada." *Sociological Inquiry* 69:575-598.

Fong, Eric, and Rima Wilkes. 1999. "The spatial assimilation model reexamined: An assessment by Canadian data." *International Migration Review* 33:594-620.

Frey, William H., and Reynolds Farley. 1996. "Latino, Asian and Black segregation in U.S. metropolitan areas: Are multiethnic metros different?" *Demography* 33:35-50.

Ginther, Donna K., Robert H. Haveman, and Barbara Schull Wolfe. 2000. "Neighborhood attributes as determinants of children's outcomes: How robust are the relationships?" *The Journal of Human Resources* 35:603-642.

Gold, Steven J. 2004. "From Jim Crow to racial hegemony: Evolving explanations of racial hierarchy." *Ethnic and Racial Studies* 27:951-968.

Gordon, Milton. 1964. *Assimilation in American life: The role of race, religion and national origins.* New York: Oxford University Press.

Guest, Avery M., and James A. Weed. 1976. "Ethnic residential segregation: Patterns of change." *American Journal of Sociology* 81:1088-1111.

Harles, John C. 2004. "Immigrant integration in Canada and the United States." *American Review of Canadian Studies* 34:223-258.

Harris, David R. 1999. ""Property values drop when blacks move in, because...":

Racial and socioeconomic determinants of neighborhood desirability."
American Sociological Review 64:461-479.

Hein, Jeremy. 1995. *From Vietnam, Laos and Cambodia: A refugee experience in the United States.* New York: Twayne Publishers.

Heisler, Barbara S. 1992. "The future of immigrant incorporation: Which models? Which concepts?" *International Migration Review* 26:623-645.

Hoffman, Diane M. 1989. "Language and culture acquisition among Iranians in the United States." *Anthropology and Education Quarterly* 20:118-132.

Holland, Kenneth M. 2007. "A history of Chinese immigration in the United States and Canada." *American Review of Canadian Studies* 37:150-160.

Hou, Feng. 2006. "Spatial assimilation of racial minorities in Canada's immigrant gateway cities." *Urban Studies* 43:1191-1213.

Iceland, John, and Melissa Scopilliti. 2008. "Immigrant residential segregation in U.S. metropolitan areas, 1990-2000." *Demography* 45:79-94.

Immergluck, Daniel. 1998. "Neighborhood economic development and local working: The effect of nearby jobs on where residents work." *Economic Geography* 74:170-187.

Itzigsohn, José. 2004. "The formation of Latino/a panethnic identities." in *Not just black and white: Historical and contemporary perspectives on immigration, race, and ethnicity in the United States,* edited by Nancy Foner and George Fredrickson. New York: Russell Sage Foundation.

Johnston, Ron, Michael Poulsen, and James Forrest. 2007a. "Ethnic and racial segregation in U.S. metropolitan areas, 1980-2000: The dimensions of segregation revisited." *Urban Affairs Review* 42:479-504.

—. 2007b. "The geography of ethnic residential segregation: A comparative study of five countries." *Annals of the Association of American Geographers* 97:713-738.

Jones, Terry-Ann. 2008. *Jamaican immigrants in the United States and Canada: Race, transnationalism and social capital.* New York: LFB Scholarly Publishing LLC.

Kalbach, Warren E. 1990. "Ethnic residential segregation and its significance for the individual in an urban setting." Pp. 92-134 in *Ethnic identity and equality: Varieties of experience in a Canadian city,* edited by R. Breton, W.W. Isajiw, W.E. Kalbach, and J.G. Reitz. Toronto: University of Toronto Press.

Kantrowitz, Nathan. 1973. *Ethnic and racial segregation in the New York metropolis: Residential patterns among white ethnic groups, blacks and Puerto Ricans.* New York: Praeger Publishers.

Kearns, Ade, and Michael Parkinson. 2001. "The significance of neighborhood." *Urban Studies* 38:2103-2110.

Kelley, Ron. 1991. "Iranian political demonstrations in Los Angeles, USA: A photographic essay." in *Iranian refugees and exiles since Khomeini,* edited by Asghar Fathi. Costa Mesa, CA: Mazda Publishers.

Kibria, Nazli. 1994. "Household structure and family ideologies: The dynamics of immigrant economic adaptation among Vietnamese refugees." *Social*

Problems 41:81-96.

Killian, Caitlin, and Karen A. Hegtvedt. 2003. "The role of parents in the maintenance of second generation Vietnamese cultural behaviors." *Sociological Spectrum* 23:213-245.

Kim, Ann H. 2007. "The flow of labour and goods in Canada's international migration system." *Canadian Studies in Population* 34:241-268.

Kim, Ann H. and Michael J. White. 2004. "Panethnicity, ethnic diversity and residential segregation." *Paper presented at the American Sociological Association, San Francisco.*

Kim, Claire Jean. 2004. "Imagining race and nation in multicultural America." *Ethnic and Racial Studies* 27:987-1005.

Kim, Sunwoong. 2000. "Race and home price appreciation in urban neighborhoods: Evidence from Milwaukee, Wisconsin." *Review of Black Political Economy* 28:9-28.

Krysan, Maria, and Reynolds Farley. 2002. "The residential preferences of blacks: Do they explain persistent segregation?" *Social Forces* 80:937-980.

Kurthen, Hermann. 1997. "Immigration and the welfare state in comparison: Differences in the incorporation of immigrant minorities in Germany and the United States." *International Migration Review* 31:721-731.

Kymlicka, Will. 1998. *Finding our way: Rethinking ethnocultural relations in Canada.* Toronto: Oxford University Press.

Lacy, Karyn R. 2004. "Black spaces, black places: Strategic assimilation and identity construction in middle-class suburbia." *Ethnic and Racial Studies* 27:908-930.

Lamba, Navjot K. 2003. "The employment experiences of Canadian refugees: Measuring the impact of human and social capital on quality of employment." *Canadian Review of Sociology and Anthropology* 40:45-64.

Langberg, Mark, and R. Farley. 1985. "Residential segregation of Asian Americans in 1980." *Sociology and Social Research* 70:71-75.

Lewin-Epstein, Noah, Noshe Semyonov, Irena Kogan, and Richard A. Wanner. 2003. "Institutional structure and immigration integration: A comparative study of immigrants' labor market attainment in Canada and Israel." *International Migration Review* 37:389-420.

Li, Peter S. 1988. *The Chinese in Canada.* Toronto: Oxford University Press.

Li, Wei. 1998. "Anatomy of a new ethnic settlement: The Chinese ethnoburb in Los Angeles." *Urban Studies* 35:479-501.

Lieberson, Stanley. 1963. *Ethnic patterns in American cities.* New York: The Free Press of Glencoe.

—. 1980. *A piece of the pie: Blacks and white immigrants since 1880.* Berkeley: University of California Press.

Light, Ivan, and Edna Bonacich. 1988. *Immigrant entrepreneurs.* Berkeley: University of California Press.

Light, Ivan Hubert, and Steven J. Gold. 2000. *Ethnic economies.* San Diego, CA: Academic Press.

Lin, Jan. 1998. *Reconstructing Chinatown: Ethnic enclave, global change.*

210 The social context of residential integration

Minneapolis: University of Minnesota Press.

Lipset, Seymour Martin. 1990. *Continental divide: The values and institutions of the United States and Canada.* New York: Routledge, Chapman and Hall, Inc.

Logan, John R., Richard D. Alba, and Wenquan Zhang. 2002. "Immigrant enclaves and ethnic communities in New York and Los Angeles." *American Sociological Review* 67:299-322.

Logan, John R., Brian J. Stults, and Reynolds Farley. 2004. "Segregation of minorities in the metropolis: Two decades of change." *Demography* 41:1-22.

Loveless, Stephen C., Clifford P. McCue, Raymond B. Surette, and Dorothy Norris-Tirrell. 1996. *Immigration and its impact on American cities.* Westport, CT: Praeger.

Lyman, Stanford M. 1974. *Chinese Americans.* New York: Random House.

Maingot, Anthony P. 1991. "Emigration and development in the English-speaking Caribbean." in *Determinants of emigration from Mexico, Central America and the Caribbean*, edited by Sergio Díaz-Briquets and Sidney Weintraub. Boulder, CO: Westview Press.

Marger, Martin N., and Constance A. Hoffman. 1992. "Ethnic enterprise in Ontario: Immigrant participation in the small business sector." *International Migration Review* 26:968-981.

Massey, Douglas S, and Brendan P Mullan. 1984. "Processes of Hispanic and Black spatial assimilation." *American Journal of Sociology* 89:836-873.

Massey, Douglas S., and Nancy A. Denton. 1985. "Spatial assimilation as a socioeconomic outcome." *American Sociological Review* 50:94-106.

—. 1987. "Trends in the residential segregation of Blacks, Hispanics, and Asians: 1970-1980." *American Sociological Review* 52:802-825.

—. 1988. "The dimensions of residential segregation." *Social Forces* 67:281-315.

Massey, Douglas S., and Mary J. Fischer. 2000. "How segregation concentrates poverty." *Ethnic and Racial Studies* 23:670-691.

Massey, Douglas S., and Eric Fong. 1990. "Segregation and neighborhood quality: Blacks, Hispanics and Asians in the San Francisco metropolitan area." *Social Forces* 69:15-32.

Massey, Douglas S., Michael J. White, and Voon-Chin Phua. 1996. "The dimensions of segregation revisited." *Sociological Methods and Research* 25:172-206.

McLean, Lorna. 2004. ""To become part of us": Ethnicity, race, literacy and the Canadian Immigration Act of 1919." *Canadian Ethnic Studies* 36:1-28.

Min, Pyong Gap. 1990. "Problems of Korean immigrant entrepreneurs." *International Migration Review* 24:436-455.

Modarres, Ali. 1992. "Ethnic community development: A spatial examination." *Journal of Urban Affairs* 14:97-107.

Modarresi, Yahya. 2001. "The Iranian community in the United States and the maintenance of Persian." *International Journal of the Sociology of*

Language 148:93-115.

Model, Suzanne. 1997. "An occupational tale of two cities: Minorities in London and New York." *Demography* 34:539-550.

Model, Suzanne, Gene Fisher, and Roxane Silberman. 1999. "Black Caribbeans in comparative perspective." *Journal of Ethnic and Migration Studies* 25:187-212.

Model, Suzanne, and David Ladipo. 1996. "Context and opportunity: Minorities in London and New York." *Social Forces* 75:485-510.

Mostofi, Nilou. 2003. "Who we are: The perplexity of Iranian-American identity." *The Sociological Quarterly* 44:681-703.

Musterd, Sako, and Sjoerd De Vos. 2007. "Residential dynamics in ethnic concentrations." *Housing Studies* 22:333-353.

Myles, John, and Feng Hou. 2004. "Changing colours: Spatial assimilation and new racial minority immigrants." *Canadian Journal of Sociology* 29:29-58.

Overman, Henry G. 2002. "Neighborhood effects in large and small neighborhoods." *Urban Studies* 39:117-130.

Park, Robert E., Ernest W. Burgess, and Roderick D. McKenzie. 1925. *The city.* Chicago: The University of Chicago Press.

Pattillo, Mary. 2005. "Black middle-class neighborhoods." *Annual Review of Sociology* 31:305-329.

Peach, Ceri. 2005. The mosaic versus the melting pot: Canada and the USA. *Scottish Geographic Journal* 121:3-27.

Portes, Alejandro (Ed.). 1995. *The economic sociology of immigration: Essays on networks, ethnicity and entrepreneurship.* New York: Russell Sage Foundation.

Portes, Alejandro, and Robert L. Bach. 1985. *Latin journey: Cuban and Mexican immigrants in the United States.* Berkeley: University of California Press.

Portes, Alejandro, and Rubén G. Rumbaut. 1996. *Immigrant America: A portrait.* Berkeley, CA: University of California Press.

—. 2001. *Legacies: The story of the immigrant second generation.* Berkeley: University of California Press.

Poulsen, Michael, Ron Johnston, and James Forrest. 2002. "Plural cities and ethnic enclaves: Introducing a measurement procedure for comparative study." *International Journal of Urban and Regional Research* 26:229-243.

Reitz, Jeffrey G. 1988. "The institutional structure of immigration as a determinant of inter-racial competition: A comparison of Britain and Canada." *International Migration Review* 22:117-146.

—. 1998. *Warmth of the welcome: The social causes of economic success in different nations and cities.* Boulder, CO: Westview Press.

— (Ed.). 2003. *Host societies and the reception of immigrants.* La Jolla, CA: Center for Comparative Immigration Studies.

Reitz, Jeffrey G., and Raymond Breton. 1994. *The illusion of difference: Realities of ethnicity in Canada and the United States.* Toronto: C.D. Howe Institute.

Reitz, Jeffrey G., Joachim R. Frick, Tony Calabrese, and Gert C. Wagner. 1999.

"The institutional framework of ethnic employment disadvantage: A comparison of Germany and Canada." *Journal of Ethnic and Migration Studies* 25:397-443.

Rekers, Ans, and Ronald van Kempen. 2000. "Location matters: Ethnic entrepreneurs and the spatial context." Pp. 54-69 in *Immigrant businesses: The economic, political and social environment*, edited by Jan Rath. Basingstoke, UK: Macmillan Press Ltd.

Robinson, W.S. 1950. "Ecological correlations and the behavior of individuals." *American Sociological Review* 15:351-357.

Schmidt, Sr., Ron. 2007. "Comparing federal government immigrant settlement policies in Canada and the United States." *American Review of Canadian Studies* 37:103-122.

Shahidian, Hammed. 1999. "Gender and sexuality among immigrant Iranians in Canada." *Sexualities* 2:189-222.

Simmons, Alan B. 1999. "Immigration policy: Imagined futures." Pp. 21-50 in *Immigrant Canada: Demographic, economic and social challenges*, edited by Shiva S. Halli and Leo Driedger. Toronto: University of Toronto Press.

Simon, Rita J., and Keri W. Sikich. 2007. "Public attitudes toward immigrants and immigration policies across seven nations." *International Migration Review* 41:956-962.

Simpson, Ludi. 2007. "Ghettos of the mind: The empirical behaviour of indices of segregation and diversity." *Journal of the Royal Statistical Society, Series A* 170:405-424.

Sjoquist, David L. 2001. "Spatial mismatch and social acceptability." *Journal of Urban Economics* 50:474-490.

Small, Mario Luis. 2007. "Racial differences in networks: Do neighborhood conditions matter?" *Social Science Quarterly* 88:320-343.

Smith, Christopher J. 1995. "Asian New York: The geography and politics of diversity." *International Migration Review* 29:59-84.

Smith, Marian L. 1998. "Immigration and Naturalization Service." in *A historical guide the U.S. government*, edited by George Thomas Kurian. New York: Oxford University Press.

Song, Miri. 2004. "Introduction: Who's at the bottom? Examining claims about racial hierarchy." *Ethnic and Racial Studies* 27:859-877.

South, J. Scott, and Kyle D. Crowder. 1997. "Escaping distressed neighborhoods: Individual, community and metropolitan influences." *American Journal of Sociology* 102:1040-1084.

Stoll, Michael A., and Steven Raphael. 2000. "Racial differences in spatial job search patterns: Exploring the causes and consequences." *Economic Geography* 76:201-223.

Taeuber, Karl E., and Alma F. Taeuber. 1964. "The Negro as an immigrant group: Recent trends in racial and ethnic segregation in Chicago." *American Journal of Sociology* 69:374-382.

—. 1965. *Negroes in cities*. Chicago: Aldine Publishing Company.

Theil, Henri, and Anthony J. Finizza. 1971. "A note on the measurement of racial integration of schools by means of informational concepts." *The Journal of Mathematical Sociology* 1:187-193.

Thomas-Hope, Elizabeth. 2002. *Caribbean migration*. Barbados: University of the West Indies Press.

Thompson, Paul, and Elaine Bauer. 2003. "Evolving Jamaican migrant identities: Contrasts between Britain, Canada and the USA." *Community, Work and Family* 6:89-102.

Timberlake, Jeffrey M., and John Iceland. 2007. "Change in racial and ethnic residential inequality in American cities, 1970-2000." *City & Community* 6:335-365.

Tubergen, Frank van, Henk Flap, and Ineke Maas. 2004. "The economic incorporation of immigrants in 18 Western societies: Origin, destination, and community effects." *American Sociological Review* 69:704-727.

Tubergen, Frank van, and Matthijs Kalmijn. 2005. "Destination-language proficiency in cross-national perspective: A study of immigrant groups in nine Western countries." *American Journal of Sociology* 110:1412-1457.

Tung, William L. 1974. *The Chinese in America 1820-1973*. Dobbs Ferry, NY: Oceana Publications, Inc.

Valtonen, Kathleen. 2004. "From the margin to the mainstream: Conceptualizing refugee settlement processes." *Journal of Refugee Studies* 17:70-96.

Waldinger, Roger. 1986. "Immigrant enterprise: A critique and reformulation." *Theory and Society* 15:249-285.

—. 1989. "Structural opportunity or ethnic advantage? Immigrant business development in New York." *International Migration Review* 23:48-72.

—. 1994. "The making of an immigrant niche." *International Migration Review* 28:3-30.

Waldinger, Roger, David McEvoy, and Howard Aldrich. 1990. "Spatial dimensions of opportunity structures." Pp. 106-130 in *Ethnic entrepreneurs: Immigrant business in industrial societies*, edited by Roger Waldinger, Howard Aldrich, Robin Ward, and Associates. Newbury Park, CA: Sage Publications, Inc.

White, Michael J. 1986. "Segregation and diversity measures in population distribution." *Population Index* 52:198-221.

White, Michael J., Eric Fong, and Qian Cai. 2003. "The segregation of Asian-origin groups in the United States and Canada." *Social Science Research* 32:148-167.

White, Michael J., and Jennifer E. Glick. 1999. "The impact of immigration on residential segregation." Pp. 345-372 in *Immigration and opportunity: race, ethnicity, and employment in the United States*, edited by Frank D. Bean and Stephanie Bell-Rose. NY: Russell Sage.

White, Michael J., Ann H. Kim, and Jennifer E. Glick. 2005. "Mapping social distance: Ethnic residential segregation in a multiethnic metro." *Sociological Methods and Research* 34:173-203.

White, Michael J., and Afaf Omer. 1997. "Segregation by ethnicity and immigrant status in New Jersey." Pp. 375-394 in *Keys to successful* immigration: Implications of the New Jersey experience, edited by Thomas J. Espenshade. Washington, DC: Urban Institute Press.

White, Michael J., and Sharon Sassler. 2000. "Judging not only by color: Ethnicity, nativity and neighborhood attainment." *Social Science Quarterly* 81:997-1013.

Winks, Robin W. 1971. *The Blacks in Canada: A history.* Montréal: McGill-Queen's University Press.

Yancey, William L., Eugene P. Ericksen, and Richard N. Juliani. 1976. "Emergent ethnicity: A review and reformulation." *American Sociological Review* 41:391-403.

Yinger, John. 1995. *Closed doors, opportunities lost: The continuing costs of housing discrimination.* New York: Russell Sage Foundation.

Zhou, Min, and Carl L. Bankston III. 1994. "Social capital and the adaptation of the second generation: The case of Vietnamese youth in New Orleans." *International Migration Review* 28:821-845.

Zhou, Min, and John R. Logan. 1991. "In and out of Chinatown: Residential mobility and segregation of New York City's Chinese." *Social Forces* 70:387-407.

Index

acculturation, 9, 44, 57-58, 77-91,
    97-99, 121, 128,
    150-151, 157-158, 162,
    193
Anglo-conformity model, 35, 53
Asian ethnic groups, 42, 48-49, 63,
    71, 83, 86-87, 90, 96,
    97-98, 102, 104,
    156-158, 162, 169, 187
Asian/East Indians, 48, 71, 76,
    153, 155, 166, 189

bilateral relations, 10, 27, 127, 165
Black ethnic groups, 42, 63, 82,
    86-87, 96-98, 105,
    156-157, 162, 189

Chicago School, 16
Chinese, 48, 71, 76, 102, 104-106,
    109, 115, 117, 121,
    129-134, 146-147,
    150-151, 155, 157, 158,
    159, 166, 189, 196
context of migration, 22-23, 41, 44,
    105, 139, 143, 147, 151,
    153-154, 163
context of reception, 10, 23
culture, 3, 16, 17, 21, 36, 126, 152,
153, 157, 159
    of migration, 102
    of moving, 38

dimensions of segregation, 56, 76,
    90
Dissimilarity Index, 53-56, 67-68,
    70-74, 76-78, 86, 90-92,
    94, 105-106, 111-112

ecological perspective, 4, 15, 21

ecological fallacy, 11, 61, 68,
    126
English, 48, 71, 166, 189
    language, See official
    language
Entropy Index, 53-56
ethnic
    ancestry, See ethnic origin
    origin, 4, 48-49, 116, 153,
        159, 187-189
    resources, 41, 57-61, 67, 69,
        77-78, 90, 96-97,
        104-105, 120, 125, 128
    retention, 9, 15, 19-21, 41-42,
        45, 77, 87, 97, 103, 128,
        135, 139, 146, 150,
        159-160

Filipinos, 48, 71, 155, 166, 189
foreign-born population, 48
French language, See official
    language

Germans, 48, 71, 155, 166, 189
group size, 49, 57, 61, 70, 78, 96,
    165

Haitians, 48, 71, 155, 166, 189
host society, 7-8, 21, 22-25, 41, 98,
    104, 162
housing, 2, 21, 23-26, 32-32,
    38-39, 61, 98, 128, 149,
    161, 192
    discrimination, 18, 38, 128
    housing market, 7, 8, 21-22,
        61, 128
    new housing, 7, 21, 61-62, 91,
        147, 149
    racial steering, 18, 24, 128

immigration policy, 23, 29-32, 39,
        44, 102, 155, 161, 173
index of dissimilarity, *See*
        Dissimilarity Index
institutional structures, 3, 15,
        23-25, 38, 162
integration policy and ideology,
        23-24, 33-35, 41, 161
    melting pot, 34-35, 97, 161
    mosaic, 34-35, 97, 161
Iranians, 48, 70, 71, 103-104, 105,
        111-113, 115, 116, 117,
        121, 138-142, 147,
        149-152, 155, 157, 159,
        166, 189, 196
Isolation Index, 53-56, 70-71, 75,
        76-77, 86, 96
Italians, 48, 71, 155, 166, 189

Jamaicans, 48, 71, 102-103, 105,
        110, 111, 115, 116, 117,
        121, 134-138, 146,
        149-151, 155, 157, 159,
        166, 189, 196

Koreans, 48, 71, 155, 166, 189

language, 3, 4, 20, 63, 105, 151
    official language, 1, 5, 30, 32,
        57-58, 78, 90, 98, 103,
        104, 152, 172-173
length of residence, 16

multiculturalism, 4
    Multiculturalism Act, 38
    multiculturalism policy, 24,
        34, 42

neighborhood context, 125

Oath of Citizenship
    U.S., 34
    Canada, 35
organizing principles, 2, 15, 23, 53

Pakistanis, 48, 71, 76, 155, 166,
        189
panethnicity, 9, 17-18, 63, 67-68,
        69, 71, 77, 82-83, 90-92,
        94-97, 105, 129, 156,
        158
place stratification, 149, 156-160
    theory, 9, 15, 19, 128-129
pluralism, 4, 35, 40
Polish, 48, 155, 166, 189
principal components analysis,
        57-58, 60
public opinion, 23, 35-36

racialized spatial assimilation, 17
refugees, 22-23, 30, 44, 104-105,
        152
religion, 4, 20-21, 25, 103, 151,
        153, 182, 192
residential
    concentration, 2-5, 9, 18,
        20-21, 26, 39, 49, 61, 87,
        97-98, 128, 146-147,
        153-154, 196
    incorporation, 15-16, 20, 40,
        41-45, 90, 97-98, 152,
        157-161, 163
    mobility, 4, 17, 22, 24, 38, 77,
        128, 151, 162
    segregation, 6, 7, 9, 15, 18-20,
        24, 42, 53-55, 68, 70-76,
        77-92, 147, 156, 159,
        161
Russians, 48, 70, 155, 166, 189

self-employment, 61, 80, 90, 96,
        121, 130, 135, 139, 143,
        146, 150, 178, 191, 196,
        202
settlement, 1, 8-10, 20-22, 25, 61,
        125
    industry, 32
    programs, 23-24, 32-33
    sector, 43, 45, 98, 161
slavery, 35

social context, 11, 147, 150
socioeconomic status, 57-58,
        77-80, 87, 90, 97-98,
        120, 128-129, 152,
        156-158, 160, 163, 193
spatial assimilation, 41-42, 44, 87,
        127-128, 130, 146,
        150-151, 156-160
    theory, 9, 15, 16-18, 20, 45,
        77
structure of inequality, 23-24,
        35-37, 39, 45, 97, 155,
        161
    class and gender, 36
    racial hierarchy, 19, 42
    racial structure, 9, 18-19, 69,
        83, 103, 160, 162

urban and regional context, 61-62,
        91-92

Vietnamese, 48, 71, 101, 104, 105,
        112, 114, 115-116, 117,
        120, 121, 142-146,
        149-153, 155, 157, 159,
        166, 189, 196

White ethnic groups, 7, 41-42, 53,
        63, 70, 82-83, 86-87, 90,
        92, 97-98, 105, 139,
        156-157